BRIDGES: Activity Guide and Assessment Options

to accompany

EFFECTIVE TEACHING METHODS
Third Edition

by
Gary D. Borich

Prepared by Debra L. Bayles

Merrill,
an imprint of Prentice Hall

Englewood Cliffs, New Jersey   Columbus, Ohio

©1996 by Prentice-Hall, Inc.
A Simon & Schuster Company
Englewood Cliffs, New Jersey 07632

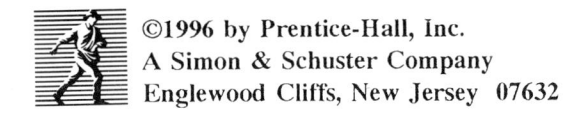

All rights reserved. Instructors of classes using Gary D. Borich, *Effective Teaching Methods,* Third Edition, may reproduce material from the activity guide for classroom use. Otherwise, no part of this book may be reproduced, in any form or by any means, without permission in writing from the Publisher.

Printed in the United States of America

10 9 8 7 6 5 4 3 2 1

ISBN: 0-02-312463-6

Special Thanks to Dottie Oliver for her work on the "Bridges" logos.

Table of Contents

INTRODUCTION..................iii
Sample Chapter Chart & References..................v
    WRITTEN CONVERSATION..................viii
    JOURNALS..................ix
    COURSE SCHEDULES..................x
    INTEREST INVENTORY..................xi

CHAPTER 1: The Effective Teacher
Teaching/Learning Ideas..................1
Checking Your Understanding..................3
Performance Assessment..................4
Children's Literature Connection..................4
References..................5
    ANTICIPATION GUIDES..................6
    THINK PAIR SHARE..................6
    MAPPING, WEBBING, GRAPHIC ORGANIZERS..................6

CHAPTER 2: Understanding Your Students
Teaching/Learning Ideas..................8
Checking Your Understanding..................10
Performance Assessment..................11
Children's Literature Connection..................13
References..................13
    CONCEPT MAP..................12
    COVERT RESPONSE TECHNIQUE..................14

CHAPTER 3: Instructional Goals and Plans
Teaching/Learning Ideas..................15
Checking Your Understanding..................17
Performance Assessment..................17
References..................18
    K-W-L..................19
    K-W-L CHART..................20

CHAPTER 4: Instructional Objectives
Teaching/Learning Ideas..................21
Checking Your Understanding..................23
Performance Assessment..................24
Children's Literature Connection..................24
References..................25
    BEHAVIORAL OBJECTIVE PLANNING SHEET..................26

CHAPTER 5: Unit and Lesson Planning
Teaching/Learning Ideas..................27
Checking Your Understanding..................29
Performance Assessment..................30
Children's Literature Connection..................30
References..................30
    WAYS TO ENHANCE INFORMATION SHARING..................33
    GAGNE LESSON PLAN FORM..................34
    HUNTER LESSON PLAN FORM..................36

CHAPTER 6: Indirect Instructional Strategies
Teaching/Learning Ideas..................38
Checking Your Understanding..................40
Performance Assessment..................41
Children's Literature Connection..................41
References..................42

CHAPTER 7: Indirect Instructional Strategies
Teaching/Learning Ideas..................43
Checking Your Understanding..................45
Performance Assessment..................46
Children's Literature Connection..................46
References..................46
    TALKING CHIPS..................47
    PARAPHRASE PASSPORT..................47
    DIRECT INSTRUCTION LESSON PLAN FORM..................48

CHAPTER 8: Questioning Strategies
Teaching/Learning Ideas..................50
Checking Your Understanding..................52

Performance Assessment 53
Children's Literature Connection 53
References.. 53
   SQ3R... 54
   MODIFIED REQUEST....................................... 54
   QARS... 55
   HOW IT WORKS (RADIO PASSAGE)................ 57

CHAPTER 9: Self-Directed Learning
Teaching/Learning Ideas... 58
Checking Your Understanding.................................. 60
Performance Assessment 61
Children's Literature Connection 61
References.. 62
   RECIPROCAL TEACHING 62
   SONG-WRITING 65
   STUDY GUIDE 66

CHAPTER 10:
Cooperative Learning and the Collaborative Process
Teaching/Learning Ideas... 67
Checking Your Understanding.................................. 69
Performance Assessment 70
References.. 70
   MOVEMENT ACTIVITY.................................... 71
   COOPERATIVE LEARNING............................. 72
      JIGSAW.. 72
      NUMBERED HEADS TOGETHER.............. 72
      ROUNDTABLE 72
      ROUNDROBIN.. 72
      TEAM WORD-WEBBING............................. 72
      STUDENT TEAMS ACHIEVEMENT DIVISIONS........ 72

CHAPTER 11: Group Process and Anticipatory Management
Teaching/Learning Ideas... 73
Checking Your Understanding.................................. 75
Performance Assessment 76

Children's Literature Connection 76
References.. 77
   CAR STORY 78
   PORCUPINE STORY 78
   ASSESSMENT ACTIVITY................................. 78
   COOPERATIVE/COLLABORATIVE PLANNING SHEET. 79
   GENERAL GUIDELINES FOR BEGINNING TEACHERS.. 80

CHAPTER 12: Classroom Order and Discipline
Teaching/Learning Ideas... 81
Checking Your Understanding.................................. 83
Performance Assessment 84
References.. 84
   RULE SONG 85
   READ-A-BOOK-IN-AN-HOUR......................... 85
   ASSESSMENT ACTIVITY................................. 85

CHAPTER 13:
Teaching Special Learners in the Regular Classroom
Teaching/Learning Ideas... 86
Checking Your Understanding.................................. 88
Performance Assessment 89
Children's Literature Connection 89
References.. 89
   GIFTED STUDENTS 91

CHAPTER 14: Assessing Learners: Objective and Essay Tests
Teaching/Learning Ideas... 93
Checking Your Understanding.................................. 95
Performance Assessment 95
References.. 96

CHAPTER 15: Assessing Learners: Performance Assessments
Teaching/Learning Ideas... 97
Checking Your Understanding.................................. 99
Performance Assessment 99
References.. 100

Introduction

Welcome to *BRIDGES*, an instructional device specially designed for instructors and students using *Effective Teaching Methods, Third Edition*. *BRIDGES* represents a new concept in textbook supplements—providing instructors and students the same lesson plans and activity ideas. As you consider its unique format, you may have questions like these:

Q: **Is *BRIDGES* a Teacher Guide or a Student Manual?**

A: Both. A traditional view of learning suggests that a teacher "teaches" information to students who "learn" it. Instructional supplements created with this view generally provide material for a teacher to share with students and/or activities for students to complete for the teacher. However, a "constructivist" view of learning suggests that students (and teachers) learn through interaction with people and materials, constructing their own personal meanings. In such views, knowledge is not something a teacher "transmits" to a student. Thus, working from the *BRIDGES* guide, instructors and students "start on the same page" to understand learning and teaching **together**, from the inside out. Students experience various strategies "as learners," and also "as teachers"—seeing from the guide how specific activities are designed and implemented, and later evaluating their effectiveness for specific purposes.

Q: **What's the best way to use *BRIDGES*?**

A: How you use *BRIDGES* depends on your teaching experience and philosophy. For example, course instructors may want to peruse the complete guide before a course begins and select specific activities to highlight in class. They may choose from among activities within a chapter, experimenting with various individual and group assignments. These learning activities can and should be viewed as experiments—and can be evaluated after their use. Related ideas and cross-references among chapters can be added as well. For example, an activity suggested in Chapter 2 may also apply to another chapter. Course instructors may also invite student input. Students can peruse the suggestions for a particular chapter and suggest activities in which they'd like to participate. They may also work on their own and select from the guide specific activities to enhance personal and small group study.

Q: **How do I assess the effectiveness of *BRIDGES* activities?**

A: The approach for course assessment varies according to the *BRIDGES* activities used in class. For example, instructors who generally implement whole class instructional approaches may desire to evaluate student progress using the true/false, multiple choice, and matching questions provided for each chapter. Those who adopt a performance assessment focus may require that students complete a personal portfolio containing a predetermined number of learning and assessment activities suggested in *BRIDGES*. These products may be supplemented with simple explanation sheets detailing why a particular product was selected for the portfolio, what was learned from the activity, and how it might apply to future learning/teaching. Other assessment ideas are also provided for each chapter.

Q: **Doesn't giving the students a copy of the Teacher's Guide detract from the freshness of the course presentation?**

A: While the answer to this question will depend largely upon your point of view, it is our belief that allowing students to see the plans from which an instructor works provides an important window on the teaching process—offering a model of how to plan and implement instruction that is often mentioned but rarely demonstrated to students. Students who are informed about possible educational interventions from which an instructor chooses, who are allowed to experience those interventions as learners, and who are allowed to share their insights about the effects of those interventions are likely to feel valued for their own expertise as learners, better internalize subtleties of particular strategies, and inform instructors of important modifications for future teaching. This dual stance on the part of instructors and students (taking both a participatory and an evaluative view) can encourage the kind of thinking necessary for reflective teaching. Further, students who see how their instructor "teaches" a course will likely gain a greater understanding of how they themselves might model specific strategies in their future classrooms.

Q: **So who's the teacher in this course?**

A: If coming to know involves constructing a personal meaning, then everyone involved in this course is both a student at times and a teacher at others. The "student" is the person who encounters something new and attempts to "fit" it into his or her existing understanding. The "teacher" is the person sharing a particular insight or idea at any given moment. This open sharing is not, however, an excuse for instructors to yield to majority rule or devalue their own experience and expertise. While a student-centered focus in instruction allows students to contribute to the learning experience, the instructor's role still remains one of guidance—there are some ideas and concepts which are more important and helpful than others, and many of these judgments (about what to focus on) should remain within the instructor's purview.

Q: **When should we read the chapters in *Effective Teaching Methods*?**

A: *BRIDGES* activities are generally written as if the chapter content has been read by all participants **before** the class meets. However, some ideas may be more effective if used before reading occurs. Additionally, some students develop strong preferences about when to read text chapters (i.e., before or after the topic is addressed in class). Instructors should peruse activity suggestions far enough in advance of a particular chapter to notify students of their preferences about when a specific chapter (or part of a chapter) should be read.

Q: **How does the format of *BRIDGES* work? What is the thinking/purpose behind each category?**

A: Instructional suggestions for each chapter are presented in chart form. Other related information appears under bold-faced headings. A sample chart with activity descriptions and references follows on pages iv-x.

Chapter Number	A. Personal, Dialogue, or Buddy Journals	B. Self-Directed Study Activities	C. Cooperative & Collaborative Ideas	D. Whole Class
Introducing the Content Assimilating /Reviewing the Content	The purpose of journal writing is to encourage students (and the instructor) to connect course concepts with personal experiences. As students express their views, they enhance their expressive capacity. Further, the process of translating mental ideas to written text can help crystalize vague ideas and reveal areas where understanding is incomplete. **DIALOGUE JOURNALS*** are generally written between the student and the instructor, **BUDDY JOURNALS** are exchanged between two student partners, and **SELF-REFLECTIVE JOURNALS** may be kept in a more traditional "diary" sense—wherein each student writes to himself/herself as the primary audience.	Ideas in this column encourage students to go beyond course requirements and extend their **own** learning. These activities provide students the freedom to work on projects at their own pace, to explore topics of interest, and to share their discoveries. The work completed in this area can be as public or as private as students desire. Indeed, some of it (or perhaps all) may never be made public.	As students interact with peers, they come to better understand one another and draw upon others' strengths to enhance their own thinking. Through carefully structured social interaction, the ability to work with others improves—yielding a sense of belonging and collegiality—which is important for affective growth and development. Throughout the course, students may work with the same partner and/or small group to achieve a sense of stability. Or, they can work with a variety of partners and small groups to gain even more experience interacting. Activities in this column should also enhance learning enjoyment as students engage in a variety of tasks, from writing song lyrics and poetry to summarizing key issues, completing art projects, etc.	Because students may come from a number of communities, they may share more differences than similarities when this course begins. As students experience course concepts and strategies together, they build a base of common experience from which to draw future examples and to support future learning. These shared experiences also build unity, broaden perspectives, and engender a sense of "groupness" and accepted norms.

*See both "REFERENCES" and "ACTIVE LEARNING" at the end of this chapter for further information about journals.

Checking Your Understanding

This is the only section of the manual in which instructor and student copies differ. While students receive the questions and answers for 10-15 practice questions per chapter, instructors receive an additional 15-20 questions and answers for use in generating a test students have not previously seen. While practice questions are not intended to "teach to the test", they do provide an example for students of the kinds of questions to expect on a traditional test, as well as suggest topic areas for test review. Teachers may want to use some practice questions in their tests along with questions from the **TEST BANK**.

Note: In cases where traditional assessment is used, it can be adapted to allow for more student input by inviting student clarification. For example, students can write in question clarifications to explain an answer. These comments could be taken into consideration in the event a student "misses" an answer—acknowledging the possibility of alternative views and readings of questions. Another adaptation (discussed in Chapter 14 of *Effective Teaching Methods*) requires students to underline and correct the false part of a true/false question to receive full credit for a correct response.

Performance Assessment Ideas

Individual	Small Group	Whole Class
This section contains suggestions for performance assessments which can be undertaken by individuals to enhance their own learning or which can be assigned by the instructor. Its goal is to enhance the application of chapter concepts to real life teaching issues and situations.	Since teachers often work in collaborative groups to evaluate curriculum and make school decisions, ideas in this section are designed to encourage cooperation and collaboration, rather than individual competitiveness. Students are evaluated not only on the quality of the group product but on the quality of group participation and interaction. Careful debriefing of these experiences can help students enhance their social and leadership skills along with their understanding of course content.	This section includes assessment options for involving the students in whole group work. Sometimes the ideas involve various assignments which students compile to create a "class" product. Other times, the ideas involve every student in completing the same experience. This differs from the first column of performance assessment ideas in that all students are required to complete a particular activity, rather than only a few. However, ideas found in Column 1 (and even Column 2) can often be interchanged with those in this column and instructors are encouraged to implement suggestions flexibly.

CHILDREN'S LITERATURE CONNECTION

Although children's literature is often regarded as something to be read and enjoyed only by young children, many instructors have found it a valuable resource for illustrating complex concepts for older audiences. Thus, this section includes children's literature sources which support course content in novel or entertaining ways. Instructors may choose to read aloud from these sources to introduce or illustrate a topic and then discuss implications with the class—or they may ask students to share from the sources and summarize connections they find between the literature and the course.

REFERENCES

These annotated references support individual study for chapter activities and concepts. For example, some references on the use of journals follow:

Anderson, Jim. (1992, 1993). Journal writing: The promise and the reality. *Journal of Reading.* 36, (4), 304-309.
   Addresses problems with journal writing such as overuse, ethics, goals, and grading. Suggests ways to make journals a useful pleasure.

Bromley, Karen. (1990). Buddy journals make the reading-writing connection. *The Reading Teacher.* 43, 2, 122-129.
   Describes the use and advantages of buddy journals.

Edwards, Phyllis R. (1991/1992). Using dialectical journals to teach thinking skills. *Journal of Reading.* 35, (4), 312-316.
   Discusses various types of journals, how to introduce them, and how to use them to encourage students' thinking skills.

Menon, Ramakrishman. (1994, June). Using mathematics journals more effectively. *Mathematics Teaching.* 18-19.
   Suggests some considerations for using journals in teaching mathematics.

Stewart, Carolyn & Chance, Lucindia. (1995). Making connections: Journal writing and the Professional Teaching Standards. *The Mathematics Teacher.* 88, (2), 92-95.
   Describes numerous ways journal writing supports mathematics instruction as well as development of other skills. Describes both teacher and student roles in journal writing.

Wells, M. Cyrene. (1992/1993). At the junction of reading and writing: How dialogue journals contribute to students' reading development. *Journal of Reading.* 36, (4), 294-302.
   A teacher studies her students' dialogue journals to determine their effect on reading development. The article includes excerpts of student entries and categories into which entries fell, along with the author's conclusions about those categories.

ACTIVE LEARNING

Methods courses are often criticized for "telling" students about approaches rather than "showing" them. To address this important concern, instructions are included in this section for completing activities **in this course** that can later be used **in elementary and secondary teaching**. Thus, students experience in this course **as learners** instructional strategies they can later use **in their own teaching**. These activities appear by name in the chapter charts, along with a page number where they are described in detail. When applicable, related articles are footnoted to the activities as well.

For example, on the first day of the college course, the instructor may invite students to complete the **WRITTEN CONVERSATION** activity explained below. This activity helps students "break the ice" on the first day and share important insights. With small adaptations, **WRITTEN CONVERSATION** can also be used by the students later when they begin teaching. Activities included throughout *BRIDGES* reflect this dual focus. They are suggested both as vehicles for college students to use **now** in learning course content—and as effective teaching strategies for college students to use **later** in teaching their own students.

WRITTEN CONVERSATION (College Adaptation)
Place students in pairs (through random assignment or by allowing them to choose someone they do not know well). Ask each student to write his or her name at the top of a blank piece of paper. Tell students that the goal of this activity is for them to discover interesting facts about one another through written conversation. As the activity begins, Student 1 writes a question for Student 2 on Student 2's paper. Student 2 does the same for Student 1. Once the question is written, they exchange papers to respond to the question in writing. Papers are then exchanged again so that a second question for Student 2 is written on Student 2's paper and vice versa. No talking is allowed during this "written conversation." Encourage students to ask not only common questions (e.g., What is your name? Why are you enrolled in this course?), but to ask creative questions (e.g., "What animal are you most like and why? What was the most exciting adventure in your life?). After approximately 5 minutes, ask students to choose two interesting insights from the interview and share them as they introduce their partners to the class.

Note: An effective extension of **WRITTEN CONVERSATION** for the first day of this course involves asking questions such as the following:

What is an effective teacher?   How do you become one?
How long does it take to become an effective teacher?   Is there only one definition of an effective teacher?

WRITTEN CONVERSATION (Elementary Adaptation)

For very young students, the teacher begins: 1) by writing questions on the chalkboard that students answer at their desks or, 2) by asking questions orally. Next, students ask the questions of one another and write or draw the responses on their papers. Students are paired and ask such questions as:

What is your name?	How old are you?	What is your favorite color?
What is your favorite food?	Do you have pets?	What do you like to do?

As above, students introduce their partners to the class and share 2-3 insights. The teacher may also take a photo of each student and add it to the "final" copy of the interview answers. This is displayed in class so students can read about each other.

JOURNALS

Journal writing encourages reflective thinking and allows students to connect personal experiences with course content. As one approach to journal writing, **PERSONAL JOURNALS** provide a safe and private avenue for student thinking—but their "diary-like" quality can also decrease their effectiveness if students fail to grasp their value, writing irregular or insincere entries. A second approach involves **DIALOGUE JOURNALS**, which allow the instructor to interact with each student on a one-to-one basis, reading and responding personally to students' emerging understandings and questions. Although the idea of responding in writing to each student can be overwhelming, instructors generally find that by responding to a few journals each day they can address each student at least once a week. While such responses require some out-of-class time to complete, benefits include the opportunity to answer students' questions as they arise and to gain insight into each student's unique perspective on course material. **BUDDY JOURNALS** fall somewhere between the privacy of personal journals and the instructor-student interaction of dialogue journals. Students address entries to a specified "buddy" in the class with whom they "correspond" daily. Buddy journals encourage student interaction and processing of course material, but provide the instructor less opportunity to engage directly in student processing (unless the instructor participates as someone's buddy).

Instructors may rely upon a particular journal approach throughout the semester, or may alternate approaches at various junctures. It is important that students know which type of journal they will be writing so that they can address their comments to an appropriate audience. Throughout the course, students should be encouraged to share personal insights from any type of journal used. Instructors should also write journal entries and share their own insights and/or struggles periodically.

Q: How should I begin the course?
A: You may want to adapt a general schedule for the course from timetables detailed below.

60 minute meeting time

Provide materials for students to make name tags as they enter. Ask them to place their name tags on the desks/tables each day for the first several days of class. You may also want students to complete (and hand in) the **INTEREST INVENTORY** (see p. xi) so you can come to know your students better. This can be done as students enter, may be assigned for "homework", or can be completed on another day.

10 minutes Introduce yourself, the course goals, and the general course outline. Take attendance if desired.
10 minutes Distribute a course syllabus, highlight key issues, ask students to read it through on their own.
5 minutes Read aloud from a children's literature source, current teaching magazine article, etc.
25 minutes Complete the **WRITTEN CONVERSATION** activity (see p. vii) to introduce students to one another and prepare for a discussion on teacher effectiveness.
10 minutes If time permits and you have chosen to use journals, introduce the idea and ask students to write a short journal entry. If not, make closing comments and dismiss the class.

90 minute meeting time

Complete the first 50 minutes as outlined on the 60 minute schedule above. Follow the schedule below for the remaining 40 minutes.

30 minutes Begin an introductory lecture, working from students' responses to the questions during the **WRITTEN CONVERSATION** activity and from suggestions on pages 1-6 of this guide.
10 minutes If time permits and you have chosen to use journals, introduce the idea and ask students to write a short journal entry. If not, make closing comments and dismiss the class.

Interest Inventory

My full name is _____ _____. My friends call me _____.	If I could have/do anything in the world, it would be _____ _____because _____.
My birthday is_____.	My favorite color is_____.
I have brothers _____ and _____ sisters. They range in age from _____ years to _____ years. My hair is _____ and my eyes are_____.	My favorite book is_____ _____. I like it because_____.
My favorite friend is _____ because_____.	When I have free time, I like to_____ _____.
The season of the year I like best is_____. I like this season best because that is when _____ _____.	My favorite subject in school is/was _____ _____ because _____ _____.
My favorite day of the week is_____. I like it because _____ _____.	My pet peeve is _____ because _____ _____.
One thing I do well is_____ _____. One thing I'd like to do better is_____ because_____.	Something I like about school is_____ _____. Something I don't like about school is _____ _____.
My experience with children and young adults includes _____ _____.	I want to be a _____ because _____.

BRIDGES

Chapter 1
The Effective Teacher

KNOWLEDGE → **ACTIVITY**

Chapter 1	A. Personal, Dialogue, or Buddy Journals	B. Self-Directed Study Activities	C. Cooperative & Collaborative Ideas	D. Whole Class
Introducing the Content	1. THINK about a favorite teacher. How did s/he act, look, teach? Why was this teacher a favorite? Did this person influence your career choice?* 2. What makes an effective teacher? What do you REMEMBER about an effective or ineffective teacher you knew? What made him/her this way?	1. Complete the practice test questions at the end of this chapter as an ANTICIPATION GUIDE (p. 6).[1] Read the chapter and then answer the questions a second time. How did your answers change? Share your experience with the class—how did it enhance your reading or involve you more in the chapter?	1. What does it mean for a teacher to be flexible? What are some memories you have of flexible or inflexible teachers? What happened? Was the outcome good or bad? Why do you feel that way? Share your responses using the cooperative learning strategy THINK, PAIR, SHARE (p. 6).[2]	1. CREATE and DISPLAY AN OVERHEAD TRANSPARENCY printed with the words "Portrait of a Perfect Teacher" and a drawing of a male or female person. With the class, BRAINSTORM attributes of a "perfect" or "effective" teacher. MAP or WEB (pp. 6-7)[2] these traits on the chalkboard or a blank overhead transparency. Encourage interaction, especially among those who differ in perspective.

*Students will need to know which type of journal they will be keeping so that they can address their comments to an appropriate audience (see p. ix).
[1]These numbers are keyed to the references and activities at the end of each chapter.

1

Chapter 1 Continued	A. Personal, Dialogue, or Buddy Journals	B. Self-Directed Study Activities	C. Cooperative & Collaborative Ideas	D. Whole Class
Assimilating /Reviewing the Content	3. **REFLECT** on a time you were praised and compare it to a time when someone extended your thinking. What were some of the affective and academic results? What differences do you see between praise and extension of thinking? 4. **REFLECT** on an unspoken classroom dialogue you remember. What seemed to be happening? What impression did you form of the participants? What conclusions did you draw?	2. **WRITE** a one or two-sentence **SUMMARY** for this chapter on the top of this page to help you remember important content at a glance. You may want to do this for every chapter as a helpful learning device.	2. Work in groups to **BRAINSTORM** ways to praise/motivate students. Think also of ways a teacher might extend short answers given by students. **SHARE** your lists with the class, and if desired, compile one class list. 3. In small groups, **ROLE PLAY** the use of praise in several impromptu student-teacher interactions. Reenact the scenarios, replacing praise with extension comments. Choose a scenario and **PERFORM** both the praise and the extension versions for the class. 4. **DISCUSS WITH A PARTNER** why teacher affect might be more important in low SES classrooms.	2. As a group, **BRAINSTORM** a definition of teaching. How does this definition relate to the discussion of the "perfect" or "effective" teacher in Activity 1-D-1 above? **COMPARE** your class definition of teaching with that in the text. How is your definition similar? How does it differ?

Chapter 1: Checking Your Understanding

True or False:

1. _____ The degree of a student's engagement with a learning task is obvious.
2. _____ If students generally complete school tasks at moderate to high rates of success, they will probably grow bored in class and suffer from a negative attitude.
3. _____ "Chapter 1" schools are those in which students have many economic and educational advantages.
4. _____ Teachers need a ready vocabulary of praise words to acknowledge and reward student effort. Some of the best of these words are: "good", "correct", and "right".
5. _____ One of the most important abilities teachers must develop is the ability to be flexible—to sense when a change from one emphasis to another is necessary.
6. _____ Studying the practices used by effective teachers is necessary to becoming an effective teacher.
7. _____ A role model definition of effective teaching followed attempts to identify psychological characteristics of effective teachers (e.g., personality, attitude, experience, and aptitude and/or achievement).
8. _____ What a teacher doesn't say is every bit as important as what a teacher does say.
9. _____ A teacher's employment experience (other than teaching) predicts little of his or her day-to-day classroom effectiveness.
10. _____ Research has identified specific teacher behaviors which consistently relate to desirable student performance.
11. _____ Teachers should ask questions for which there is a single "right" answer most of the time.
12. _____ The use of different instructional materials, displays, and activities within the same lesson generally overwhelms students.
13. _____ There is a large body of research about the effects of SES (socioeconomic status) on the educational achievement of students at the secondary level.
14. _____ Students feel important and are encouraged to participate in class when a teacher uses their ideas in moving a class lecture or activity forward.

| 1. F | 2. F | 3. F | 4. F | 5. T | 6. T | 7. F |
| 8. T | 9. T | 10. T | 11. F | 12. F | 13. F | 14. T |

Chapter 1: Performance Assessment Ideas

Individual	Small Group	Whole Class
1. **REFER BACK** to your journal entry for activity 1-A-2. What traits did you list in your description of an effective teacher? How many of these traits are mentioned in Chapter 1 of your text? Are there traits you'd add to that list? Delete? Why? **SUPPORT** your views with appropriate sources (including personal experience, text passages, and other sources). 2. **CHOOSE** an activity from this guide (or from activities you brainstorm to accompany this chapter). Complete a short **SUMMARY** page which includes the goal of the activity, what you learned from participating in it, and the rationale for including this activity product in your portfolio.*	1. Work in groups according to your area of teaching interest to **CREATE A WRITTEN PROFILE** of an effective teacher (in general terms). Support the profile with citations from your course text or other appropriate sources. **PRESENT** your profile to the class and request their feedback. **MAKE CHANGES** you feel are warranted.	1. Work as a class to **WRITE A SUMMARY** of important aspects of this chapter for quick reference in the future. You may want each class member to review a particular page or chapter section and write a one-sentence summary. **COMBINE** each sentence summary (in order), **DUPLICATE**, and **SHARE** with class members.*

*This suggestion may be implemented with individuals, pairs, small groups, or the whole class and can be used for any chapter.

CHILDREN'S LITERATURE CONNECTION

Brown, Marc. (1976). *Arthur's nose.* **Boston: Little, Brown & Co. (ISBN 0-316-11070)**
There's much more to Arthur than his physical appearance, as is true with all students.

Prelutsky, Jack. (1983). *The Random House book of poetry for children.* **New York: Random House. (ISBN 0-394-85010-6)**
Includes a wide variety of tried and true children pleasers. "Rules" poem by Karla Kuskin appears on p. 137.

Van Loan, Nancy. (1990). *Possum come a-knockin'.* New York: Alfred A. Knopf, Inc. (ISBN 0-679-83468-0)
This delightful story with rhythmic language offers a chance to view diverse communities and home life experiences in a rich way. May also help students realize that coming to know their students may be much like spotting a possum at the door: We must REALLY look to know and understand what we see.

REFERENCES

[2]Baumann, James F. & Johnson, Dale D. (1984). Reading instruction and the beginning teacher: A practical guide. Minneapolis, MN: Burgess Publishing Company.
Offers instructions for completing semantic mapping and semantic feature analysis along with numerous examples.

Clarke, John H. (1991). Using visual organizers to focus on thinking. *Journal of Reading.* 34, (7), 526-534.
Offers explanations and examples of several visual organizers and describes how their use can enhance student learning and thinking.

[1]Duffelmeyer, Frederick A. (1994). Effective Anticipation Guide statements for learning from expository prose. *Journal of Reading.* 37, (6), 452-457.
Gives examples of effective and ineffective statements for Anticipation Guides.

Larson, C.O. & Danswereau, D. F., (1986). Cooperative learning in dyads. *Journal of Reading.* 29, 516-520.
Offers ideas for cooperative learning activities in pairs.

Ruddell, Robert B. (1995). Those influential literacy teachers: Meaning negotiators and motivation builders. *The Reading Teacher.* 48, (6), 454-463.
Discusses characteristics of influential and motivating educators, and includes 10 instructional insights drawn from such teachers.

Toumasis, Charalampos. (1995). Concept worksheet: An important tool for learning. The Mathematics Teacher. 88, (2), 98-100.
Stresses how visual representations help students better understand mathematics concepts. Includes samples of a proposed worksheet format to help students visualize mathematics concepts.

Vaughn, Sharon; Schumm, Jeanne Shay; Niarhos, Frances Johnson; & Gordon, Jane. (1993). Students' perceptions of two hypothetical teachers' instructional adaptations for low achievers. *Elementary School Journal.* 94, (1), 87-102.
A majority of elementary students studied preferred teachers who made adaptations for individual student needs. High achievers were more supportive of teachers who individualized than were low achievers. The authors suggest that perhaps low achievers value inclusion, fitting in, and being "treated the same as the others" over instructional adaptations that single them out as having learning difficulties.

Weir, Robert E. (1994). A picture's worth a thousand words. Using models to demystify secondary social studies writing. *The Social Studies.* 85, (3), 134-137.
Notes that essay formats can be depicted visually to help students better understand how to write social studies information.

ACTIVE LEARNING

ANTICIPATION GUIDES look somewhat like a traditional test, but include two answer columns. One column is labeled "BEFORE READING" and the other is labeled "AFTER READING". Drawing upon prior knowledge and experience, students answer each question before reading a particular text. The questions are generally written in a true/false format, but can also be multiple choice or fill-in. After students answer the questions, they read the text to see how their answers compare to the information in the text. They then return to the questions and answer them a second time (in the "AFTER READING" column), making notes about the changes as desired. Students then discuss the "correct" answers as a group. Note: This activity is especially effective if some of the questions are open-ended enough to encourage broad discussion and sharing of personal opinion and experience.

THINK PAIR SHARE is a dyad activity in which students work in pairs to complete a learning task. First they consider a question on their own for a minute or two, perhaps jotting notes about their ideas. Then they meet with a partner to compare ideas and come up with a summary of the two ideas (usually within a limited time period, e.g., 2-5 minutes). Each pair then shares its response with another pair of students (making a square) or with the class as a whole. (Note: Shy partners can be involved by asking partners to share ideas they liked, e.g., "Think of something your partner said and share that with the group.")

MAPPING, WEBBING and other **GRAPHIC ORGANIZER TECHNIQUES** are visual illustrations of ideas and concepts, such as flow charts, pie charts, and family trees. The following chart (p. 7) includes four commonly used forms and their purposes (from which you may wish to choose during the course):

Four Types of Graphic Organizers

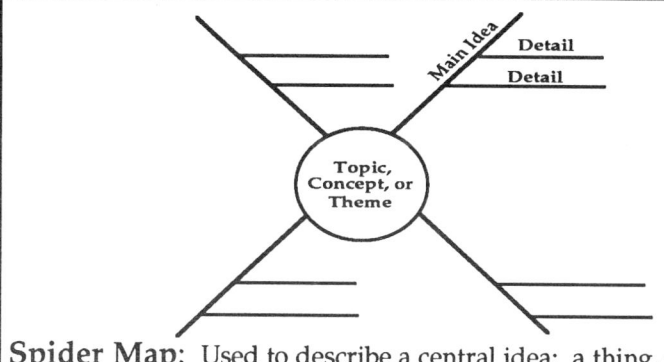

Spider Map: Used to describe a central idea: a thing, process, concept, or proposition with support. Key frame questions: What is the central idea? What are its attributes? What are its functions?

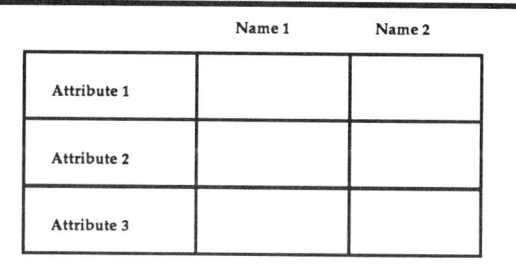

Comparison Matrix: Used to show similarities and differences between two things (e.g., people, places, events, ideas, etc.). Key frame questions: What things are being compared? How are they similar? How are they different?

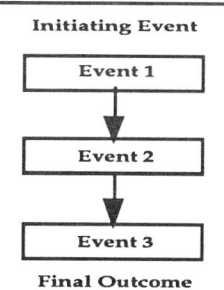

Series of Events Chain: Used to describe the stages of something; the steps in a linear procedure; a sequence of events; or the goals, actions, and outcomes of a historical figure or character in a novel. Key frame questions: What is the object, procedure, or initiating event? What are the stages or steps? How do they lead to one another? What is the final outcome?

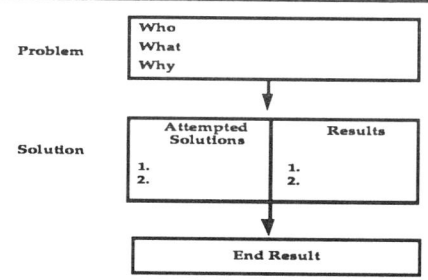

Problem-Solution Frame: Used to represent a problem, attempted solutions, and results. Key frame questions: What was the problem? Who had the problem? Why was it a problem? What attempts were made to solve the problem? Did those attempts succeed?

Jones, B.F.; Pierce, J.; & Hunter, B. (1989). Teaching students to construct graphic representations. *Educational Leadership*. 46 (4), 20-25.

BRIDGES

KNOWLEDGE — **ACTIVITY**

Chapter 2
Understanding Your Students

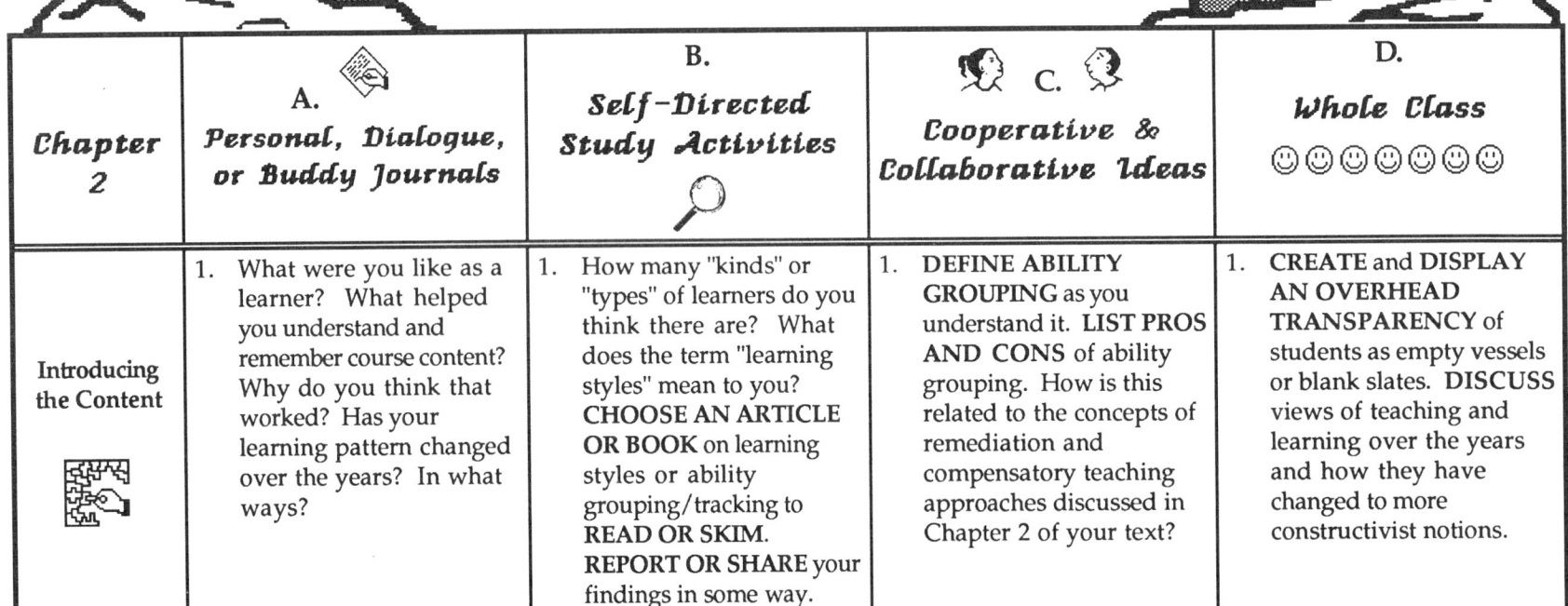

Chapter 2	A. Personal, Dialogue, or Buddy Journals	B. Self-Directed Study Activities	C. Cooperative & Collaborative Ideas	D. Whole Class
Introducing the Content	1. What were you like as a learner? What helped you understand and remember course content? Why do you think that worked? Has your learning pattern changed over the years? In what ways?	1. How many "kinds" or "types" of learners do you think there are? What does the term "learning styles" mean to you? **CHOOSE AN ARTICLE OR BOOK** on learning styles or ability grouping/tracking to **READ OR SKIM**. **REPORT OR SHARE** your findings in some way.	1. **DEFINE ABILITY GROUPING** as you understand it. **LIST PROS AND CONS** of ability grouping. How is this related to the concepts of remediation and compensatory teaching approaches discussed in Chapter 2 of your text?	1. **CREATE** and **DISPLAY AN OVERHEAD TRANSPARENCY** of students as empty vessels or blank slates. **DISCUSS** views of teaching and learning over the years and how they have changed to more constructivist notions.

Chapter 2 Continued	A. Personal, Dialogue, or Buddy Journals	B. Self-Directed Study Activities	C. Cooperative & Collaborative Ideas	D. Whole Class
Assimilating /Reviewing the Content	2. REFLECT on a time when a teacher failed or succeeded in adapting course content to your background. What happened? Why? How could this experience have been enhanced or avoided? 3. How might your journal entries for this course relate to the concept of becoming a reflective teacher as discussed in Chapter 1 of your text? How might these ideas relate to your future students?	2. MAKE A LIST of your perceived strengths and weaknesses in becoming a teacher. How do they relate to those in the text? 3. WRITE A SHORT PROFILE of a student you have known (or one you expect to meet). Suggest remediation/compensatory teaching ideas for adapting to that learner's needs. 4. How does home influence, peer pressure, or television viewing relate to academic achievement? READ OR SKIM 2-3 SOURCES dealing with one of these topics. Did your opinion change as a result of your research? REPORT OR SHARE your findings in some way.	2. DISCUSS WITH A PARTNER: What is intelligence? Can intelligence be "taught"? 3. THINK OF A VISUAL WAY TO DEPICT THE IDEA of multiple intelligences. SHARE the finished product with the class. 4. Think of a specific curriculum concept and BRAINSTORM how that concept might be adapted/expanded to include some of the multiple intelligence ideas. SHARE your ideas with the class through a ROLE PLAY or other appropriate means.	2. Use practice questions from the chapter to complete a COVERT RESPONSE TECHNIQUE (p. 14). DEBRIEF on the value of this technique. 3. BRAINSTORM influences on learning and categorize. MAP (pp. 6-7) and COMPARE to the text discussion. 4. Introduce the CONCEPT MAP (see p. 12) as an overhead transparency. Trace the ideas with students and discuss how a concept map can enhance understanding.

Chapter 2: Checking Your Understanding

True or False:

1. _____ Social class is a much less important factor in educational achievement than is race/ethnicity.
2. _____ Personality traits are stable across children and rarely vary according to race or culture.
3. _____ The practice of ability grouping can actually increase differences in academic performance between groups.
4. _____ Psychologists like Erikson suggest that certain aspects of personality develop or dominate at certain periods in our lives. This idea is important for teachers so they can plan ways to teach other personality traits to students.
5. _____ Teachers must adjust both content and their teaching practices to the average student in the classroom.
6. _____ According to Sternberg, one's ability to adapt to the environment may be a helpful measure of one's intelligence.
7. _____ Personality is a relatively benign factor in educational achievement.
8. _____ Adaptive teaching means to apply the same instructional strategy to different groups of learners so that all students experience each strategy.
9. _____ Although learning is influenced by several layers or systems, the systems view offers little practical information for day-to-day instructional planning.
10. _____ Some researchers and educators believe that intelligence can be influenced through instruction in specific areas.
11. _____ Compensatory instruction is designed to help a student gain needed information or skills in order to benefit from planned instruction.
12. _____ According to environmentalist thinking, the effect of one's home environment upon one's IQ is at least as important as heredity.
13. _____ Students from low SES (socioeconomic status) homes have generally had a good deal of experience with the same kinds of activities that go on at school.
14. _____ The conditions teachers need to consider for teaching are: curriculum, learning objectives, instructional materials, and learners.
15. _____ Students need successful horizontal relationships so they can compare themselves with others.
16. _____ It is more important to know a student's general ability and intelligence rather than his or her specific aptitudes.
17. _____ All anxiety interferes with learning.
18. _____ Some researchers claim that humans have specialized abilities which influence general performance.

1. F	2. F	3. T	4. F	5. F	6. T	7. F	8. F	9. F
10. T	11. T	12. T	13. F	14. T	15. F	16. F	17. F	18. T

Chapter 2: Performance Assessment Ideas		
Individual	**Small Group**	**Whole Class**
1. **LIST AND EXPLAIN** 2-3 alternatives to ability grouping for meeting special needs of students. How or why are these alternatives desirable? 2. **CREATE A CONCEPT MAP** (like the one on p. 12) for another course assignment and use it for studying the content. Write a short **SUMMARY** of how the map helped you (or failed to help you) in your study. Include a copy of the map with your summary.	1. **REFLECT** on how your group work in this course has been similar to or different from ability grouping contexts. **WRITE** your ideas in the form of a short essay, a persuasive poem, or other communicative device (see p. 33 for a list of ideas).*	1. Obtain a description of students' abilities in a particular subject and grade from a teacher currently teaching. As a class, **BRAINSTORM** suggestions for grouping strategies this teacher might use to meet the learning needs of the students. **WRITE** up your final ideas and submit to the teacher. (You may want to break into small groups for the writing portion of this experience.)

*Many assessment ideas will apply across chapters, so you may also want to review previous (and forthcoming) assessment ideas.

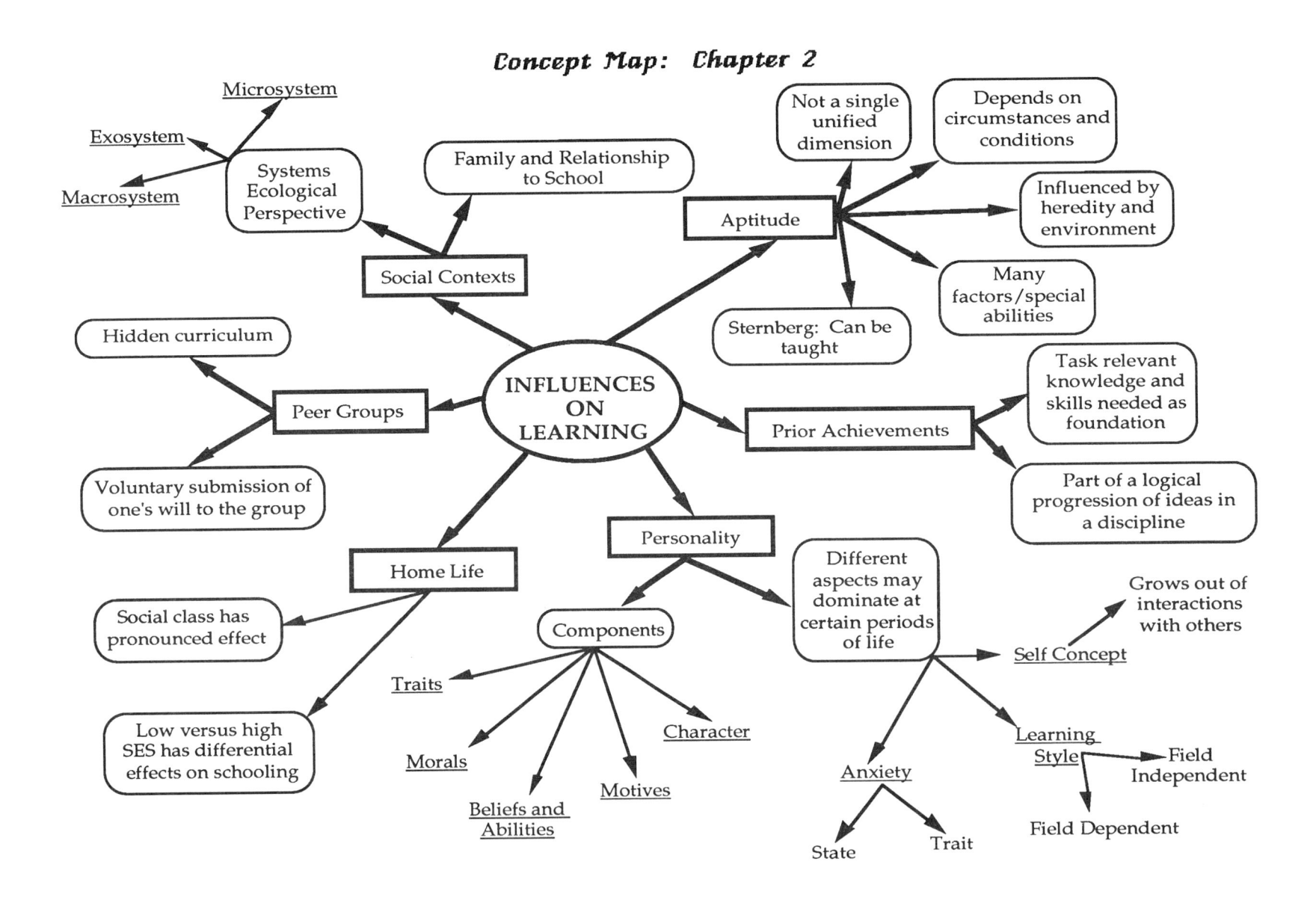

Concept Map: Chapter 2

INFLUENCES ON LEARNING

- **Social Contexts**
  - Systems Ecological Perspective
    - Microsystem
    - Exosystem
    - Macrosystem
  - Family and Relationship to School

- **Aptitude**
  - Not a single unified dimension
  - Depends on circumstances and conditions
  - Influenced by heredity and environment
  - Many factors/special abilities
  - Sternberg: Can be taught

- **Peer Groups**
  - Hidden curriculum
  - Voluntary submission of one's will to the group

- **Prior Achievements**
  - Task relevant knowledge and skills needed as foundation
  - Part of a logical progression of ideas in a discipline

- **Home Life**
  - Social class has pronounced effect
  - Low versus high SES has differential effects on schooling

- **Personality**
  - Components
    - Traits
    - Morals
    - Beliefs and Abilities
    - Motives
    - Character
  - Different aspects may dominate at certain periods of life
    - Self Concept
      - Grows out of interactions with others
    - Anxiety
      - State
      - Trait
    - Learning Style
      - Field Independent
      - Field Dependent

12

Lobel, Arnold. (1982). *Ming Lo moves the mountain.* New York: Scholastic. (ISBN 0-590-42902-7)
Just as Ming Lo achieves his goals step by step, so teachers achieve planning skill and instructional success in a step by step manner.

REFERENCES

Bintz, William P. (1995). Reflections on teaching in multicultural settings. *The Social Studies.* 86, (1), 39-42.
Suggests that education models should be based on the need for diversity rather than similarity among students.
Bullock, Janis. (1993, November). Shy kids: Don't shy away. *Education Digest.* 57-58.
Suggests that most "shy" children are not at-risk and will overcome the shyness over time.
Davey, Beth. (1989). Active responding in content classrooms. *Journal of Reading.* 33, (1), 44-46.
Summarizes several ways three multiple response techniques can be used before, during, and after reading (can be applied to other subjects).
Dollase, Richard. (1992). *Voices of beginning teachers.* New York: Teachers College Press.
Offers an in-depth look at four beginning teachers which may be especially thought-provoking for prospective teachers.

CHILDREN'S LITERATURE CONNECTION

Flood, James; Lapp, Diane; Flood, Sharon; & Nagel, Greta. (1992). Am I allowed to group? Using flexible patterns for effective instruction. *The Reading Teacher.* 45, (8), 608-616.
Discusses the history of ability grouping and describes effective grouping patterns. Advocates the use of flexible grouping patterns in reading instruction. Ideas can be adapted to other subject instruction as well.
Huber, Tonya. (1992). Culturally responsible pedagogy: "The case of Josefina Guzman." *Teaching Education.* 5, (1), 123-131.
Describes how one teacher comes to know and meet her students' needs.
Jackson, Francesina R. (1993/1994). Seven strategies to support a culturally responsive pedagogy. *Journal of Reading.* 37, (4), 298-303.
Offers seven areas for teachers to consider in becoming more culturally sensitive.
Kreidler, William J. (1995, January/February). Say good-bye to bias. *Instructor.* 28.
Describes several activities to embrace diversity within the classroom.
Marshall, Patricia L. (1995, March). Misconceiving multicultural education. *Education Digest.* 57-60.
Challenges four common misconceptions about multicultural education.
Nathan, Ruth. (1995). Parents, projects, and portfolios: 'Round and about community building in Room 14. *Language Arts.* 72, (2), 82-87.
A third-grade teacher shares her experiences in implementing portfolio assessment, completing projects, and involving parents in her classroom.

Purcell-Gates, Victoria; L'Allier, Susan, & Smith, Dorothy. (1995). Literacy at the Harts' and the Larsons': Diversity among poor, inner city families. *The Reading Teacher.* 48, (7), 572-578.
  Notes the wide variation in how family members use print in the home.

Smith, Elizabeth Meier. (1992). Answering the voices in my head: Students and teachers can make a difference. *The Reading Teacher.* 45, (6), 424-427.
  A first-year teacher shares her experience in mixing up ability groups.

Wood, Karen D. & Muth, K. Denise. (1991). The case for improved instruction in the middle grades. *Journal of Reading.* 35, (2), 84-90.
  Notes the differences in middle schools and suggests instructional formats to better meet the special needs of students this age.

ACTIVE LEARNING

In the **COVERT RESPONSE TECHNIQUE** the teacher poses a question and asks students to respond by holding up some sort of private signal (thumbs up, "yes" or "no" cards, etc.) that only the teacher can see. In this way, students demonstrate their understanding of a concept in a nonevaluative, risk-free environment. Seeing all the responses allows the teacher to immediately assess student understanding and determine the next instructional step.

BRIDGES

KNOWLEDGE — **ACTIVITY**

Chapter 3
Instructional Goals and Plans

Chapter 3	A. Personal, Dialogue, or Buddy Journals	B. Self-Directed Study Activities	C. Cooperative & Collaborative Ideas	D. Whole Class ☺☺☺☺☺☺
Introducing the Content	1. What concerns you most about becoming a teacher? How do you plan to deal with your concern(s)?	1. What comes to your mind when you think of goals and plans? Are these useful to you in your personal growth? How might your knowledge and experience with goals and plans enhance/inhibit your work as a teacher seeking to organize curriculum?	1. What are some educational biases you've experienced or observed? What were the effects of these? How might they be altered? 2. **DISCUSS THE FOLLOWING QUESTIONS** in a small group or with a partner: Can you teach someone to think? How? Why or why not?	1. Complete a **K-W-L** activity (pp. 19-20)[1] before reading or discussing the chapter: What do we know about goals and plans for teaching? What do we want to know? 2. **HOLD A DEBATE**[2] on whether you can teach someone to think. Assign teams to support and challenge the idea and plan a structured format for sharing these ideas in class.

15

Chapter 3 Continued	A. Personal, Dialogue, or Buddy Journals	B. Self-Directed Study Activities	C. Cooperative & Collaborative Ideas	D. Whole Class
Assimilating /Reviewing the Content	2. COMPARE the concept of a "thinking" curriculum (in your text) with your own school experiences. 3. How do you feel about a "standard" or "set" curriculum as opposed to a more flexible, open approach? What advantages or disadvantages do you see in outlining curriculum carefully and in detail?	2. COMPLETE THE CONCERNS CHECKLIST in your class text now and at the end of the course. What did you discover about yourself and your concerns over time? 3. How will your emotional needs be met when you are teaching? What concerns do you have about your own students' needs for emotional support? What can/should you do to support them? Consider a poetic response here, or perhaps a humorous look at ways to survive the stresses of teaching.[3]	3. BRAINSTORM related terms for the words "behavior," "conditions," and "proficiency." MAP the terms and ideas (pp. 6-7) for each of the three words. Talk about why good behavioral objectives must include all three ideas. 4. MAP Chapter 3 or a key part of the chapter (pp. 6-7). Make your map into a recipe or graphic of some sort and EXPLAIN it to the class. 5. In groups, BRAINSTORM some community values common to a specific setting. How might these influence teaching goals and plans? How can a teacher become aware of these if s/he begins teaching in an unfamiliar setting?	3. BRAINSTORM the meaning of the terms "aims," "goals," "objectives." Where does curriculum come from and what should be taught? How should it be taught (planning)?

Chapter 3: Checking Your Understanding

Match the following terms with your own definitions or summary statements taken from the text:

aims	thinking curriculum	tacit knowledge	systematic bias
goals	planning	reflection	self concerns
objectives	decisions	generating alternatives	task concerns
memorization	learner characteristics	eliminating bias	impact concerns

Performance Assessment Ideas

Individual	Small Group	Whole Class
1. Obtain a copy of the curriculum guide for a grade/setting in which you would like to teach. **REVIEW** its contents and **WRITE A REACTION** to it. What do you see as strengths? Weaknesses? What ideas for teaching units come to your mind? 2. **READ** the article by Cornbleth[4] and **RESPOND** to her points about influences on curriculum. What groups or viewpoints appear most strongly represented in the curriculum taught in the schools in your area? How do you feel about this?	1. Obtain a copy of a curriculum guide for a specific subject area or grade level you'd like to teach. Meet with a small group of others with similar interests and **CRITIQUE THE GUIDE'S CONTENTS**. What important ideas/connections do you see in the guide? What might you alter? Why? Do you see evidence of a "thinking curriculum" emphasis in the guide?	1. Work in small groups to **GENERATE** scenarios about which teachers may feel concern (e.g., discipline issues, teaching difficulties, etc.). It is best if the scenarios are drawn from actual events and experiences. **COPY** and **SHARE** the scenarios. Hold a class **DISCUSSION** regarding ways to solve each of the scenario problems. At its conclusion, **ASK** class members to **EVALUATE** the usefulness of the activity and **WRITE** about how it affected their professional growth and understanding.

Remember to review assessment suggestions for all other chapters—many ideas will apply throughout the course.

REFERENCES

Beed, Penny L.; Hawkings, E. Marie; & Roller, Cathy M. (1991). Moving learners toward independence: The power of scaffolded instruction. *The Reading Teacher.* 44, (9), 648-655.
   Discusses the constructivist concept of scaffolding and describes how it can be accomplished in numerous ways in teaching.

[2]Butz, Carol S. (1995). Great debate! *The Reading Teacher.* 48, (7), 618-619.
   Describes her own experience in setting up a third grade debate which can be adapted to many other settings.

[4]Cornbleth, Catherine. (1995). Controlling curriculum knowledge: Multicultural politics and policymaking. *Journal of Curriculum Studies.* 27, (2), 165-185.
   Describes some of the arguments in New York about a multicultural social studies curriculum. Observes that there are numerous influences on what is chosen as approved curriculum.

Littledyke, M. (1994). Primary teacher responses to the National Curriculum for Science. *The School Science Review.* 75, (273), 106-116.
   Although slightly technical in style, this article offers a helpful summary of how primary teachers view their science instruction.

[3]McVeigh-Schultz, Jane. (1995). Poetry and assessment. *Language Arts.* 72, (1), 39-41.
   Suggests that having students create poetry can provide a fresh assessment tool.

Miholic, Vincent. (1994). An inventory to pique students' metacognitive awareness of reading strategies. *Journal of Reading.* 38, (2), 84-86.
   Provides a short questionnaire students can complete (from junior high through college age) to become more aware of metacognitive reading strategies they use and may want to learn.

Monson, Robert J. & Monson, Michele Pahl. (1994). Literacy as inquiry: An interview with Jerome C. Harste. *The Reading Teacher.* 47, (7), 518-521.
   Harste, a well-known reading educator, suggests that the curriculum of the future can and should be based on student-generated inquiry.

Shanks, Joyce. (1994). Students' reactions to a standardized curriculum: A case study. *Journal of Curriculum and Supervision.* 10, (1), 43-59.
   Describes the change in viewpoint among teachers and students when Burr Oaks Elementary adopted a standardized, textbook-based curriculum. Definitions of learning narrowed and teachers felt hampered in meeting students' individual needs.

[1]Sippola, Arne E. (1995). K-W-L-S. *The Reading Teacher.* 48, (6), 542-543.
   Suggests an additional column on the traditional K-W-L chart for "What I still need to learn."

Wanko, Michael A. (1995, March). Cut stress now. *Education Digest.* 40-41.
   Offers practical strategies for teachers to decrease job stress.

ACTIVE LEARNING

K-W-L is an instructional strategy where the teacher uses brainstorming and direct questioning with the whole class to determine what they **KNOW** (K) about the content from prior instruction and personal experiences. Ask students what they already know about the topic. List all ideas the students generate (correct or incorrect). Note disagreements and questions in the center column as questions to be answered and things they **WANT** (W) to learn. Students read to answer their questions, jotting down information and new questions that arise. (You may even have students read to answer their own personal questions they write.) After reading, students articulate what they have **LEARNED** (L) and what they still need to learn. Remaining questions may be used for further research and inquiry.

Ogle, D. (1986). K-W-L: A teaching model that develops active reading of expository text. *The Reading Teacher*. 39, 564-571.

K-W-L Chart

What We KNOW (K)	What We WANT to Find Out (W)	What We LEARNED (L)

BRIDGES

KNOWLEDGE — **ACTIVITY**

Chapter 4
Instructional Objectives

Chapter 4	A. *Personal, Dialogue, or Buddy Journals*	B. *Self-Directed Study Activities*	C. *Cooperative & Collaborative Ideas*	D. *Whole Class* ☺☺☺☺☺☺
Introducing the Content	1. What has happened/what do you mean when you say you have "learned" something? How do you learn best? What makes it hard for you to learn something? 2. Are there universals that help everyone learn? If you think so, what are some of these?	1. **REFLECT** on the author's claim that behavioral objectives need a goal, conditions, and criteria to be effective. Is this so? Why or why not?	1. In groups, **DISCUSS** the following question: What is it that behavioral objectives do for teachers?	1. **DISPLAY A VISUAL** of Escher's staircase or other optical illusion where the eye seems to keep moving yet fails to progress. Discuss how well-conceived and well-written behavioral objectives help teachers achieve more than just an "illusion" of progress.

Chapter 4 Continued	A. Personal, Dialogue, or Buddy Journals	B. Self-Directed Study Activities	C. Cooperative & Collaborative Ideas	D. Whole Class
Assimilating /Reviewing the Content	3. The acronym "K.I.S.S." sometimes stands for "Keep it simple, stupid." How might this mnemonic be helpful when considering writing and use of behavioral objectives?	2. RESPOND to the idea that learning must be accompanied by a change in behavior. Do you agree or disagree? Why? 3. WRITE 2-3 intentionally vague or "bad" behavioral objectives for Activity 4-C-2.	2. Work in pairs with poorly written behavioral objectives to CORRECT and SHARE them (can be chosen from those created in activity 4-B-3). Use the BEHAVIORAL OBJECTIVE PLANNING SHEET (p. 26) to help you improve the objectives. 3. How can/should teachers set criterion levels for behavioral objectives? How could/should criterion levels change over time?	2. BRAINSTORM with the group what it means to "learn" something. How do you know it's been learned? 3. DISCUSS the BEHAVIORAL OBJECTIVE PLANNING SHEET (p. 26) with the class and describe the importance of the three areas in writing useful behavioral objectives.

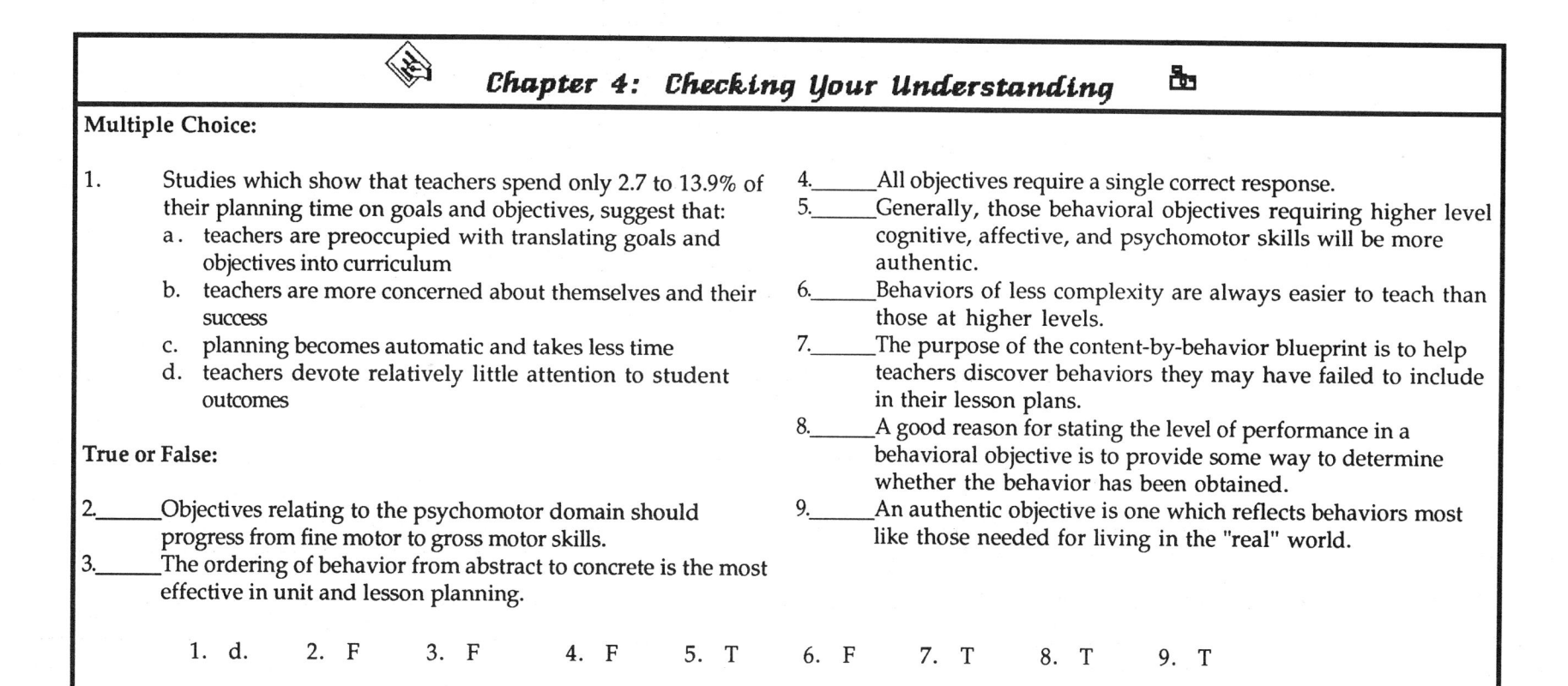

Chapter 4: Checking Your Understanding

Multiple Choice:

1. Studies which show that teachers spend only 2.7 to 13.9% of their planning time on goals and objectives, suggest that:
   a. teachers are preoccupied with translating goals and objectives into curriculum
   b. teachers are more concerned about themselves and their success
   c. planning becomes automatic and takes less time
   d. teachers devote relatively little attention to student outcomes

True or False:

2. _____ Objectives relating to the psychomotor domain should progress from fine motor to gross motor skills.
3. _____ The ordering of behavior from abstract to concrete is the most effective in unit and lesson planning.
4. _____ All objectives require a single correct response.
5. _____ Generally, those behavioral objectives requiring higher level cognitive, affective, and psychomotor skills will be more authentic.
6. _____ Behaviors of less complexity are always easier to teach than those at higher levels.
7. _____ The purpose of the content-by-behavior blueprint is to help teachers discover behaviors they may have failed to include in their lesson plans.
8. _____ A good reason for stating the level of performance in a behavioral objective is to provide some way to determine whether the behavior has been obtained.
9. _____ An authentic objective is one which reflects behaviors most like those needed for living in the "real" world.

1. d.　2. F　3. F　4. F　5. T　6. F　7. T　8. T　9. T

Chapter 4:	*Performance Assessment Ideas*	
Individual	*Small Group*	*Whole Class*
1. **WRITE** 2-3 behavioral objectives for an imaginary class. **SUPPORT** your choice of words and instructional strategies from appropriate sources. 2. **CONTACT** a local school district and **DETERMINE** the suggested time allocations per subject for a grade level you'd like to teach (i.e., 45 minutes daily for mathematics, etc.). **CHART** your findings and **RESPOND** to the suggestions. What would you alter? Why?	1. Work in groups to **REVISE** the **BEHAVIORAL OBJECTIVE PLANNING SHEET** (p. 26) in some way to make it more useful for you. **SHARE** your revisions with class members, and support your changes from appropriate sources.	1. **BRAINSTORM** some things you have learned in this course. Individually or in small groups, divide this list and create behavioral objectives that could have supported this learning. Share your ideas with class members and make appropriate changes.

CHILDREN'S LITERATURE CONNECTION

Zolotow, Charlotte. (1989). *Someday.* **New York: Harper Trophy. (ISBN 0-06-443207-6).**
Ellen dreams of all the wonderful things that will happen "someday"—a little like the big teaching goals and plans we must sometimes downsize to make attainable.

Shorto, Russell. (1990). *Cinderella: The untold story.* **New York: Carol Publishing Group. (ISBN 1-55972-0054-9)**
Cinderella's sister has a slightly different view of the well-known story. Just as she offers a different perspective, it can be helpful to view our curriculum goals and approaches from more than one perspective, since choosing what to emphasize also means choosing things to overlook or deemphasize.

REFERENCES

Campbell, Jim. (1994). Managing the primary curriculum: The issue of time allocation. *Education 3-13.* 22, (1), 3-13.
  Discusses time allocated to each subject and teachers' views of the adequacy of those allocations.

Schwartz, Sydney. (1995). Authentic mathematics in the classroom. *Teaching Children Mathematics.* 1, (9), 580-584.
  Offers a number of ideas for teachers of young children to link daily school activities with real life and mathematics.

Smith, J. Lea & Johnson, Holly. (1994). Models for implementing literature in content studies. *The Reading Teacher.* 48, (3), 198-209.
  Presents a framework for understanding and developing various types of literature-based units.

Uhrmacher, P. Bruce. (1993). Coming to know the world through Waldorf Education. *Journal of Curriculum and Supervision.* 9, (1), 87-104.
  Describes Waldorf education, an approach to teaching where students learn content subjects largely through artistic activities. Stresses that Waldorf teachers rely on powerful pedagogical tools often neglected by the general education community.

Vacc, Nancy Nesbitt; Ervin, Criss; & Travis, Sue. (1995). Implementing the professional standards for teaching mathematics. Beyond the classroom. *Teaching Children Mathematics.* 1, (8), 494-497.
  Goes beyond daily objectives to link real-life activities with curriculum goals and learners of different ages.

Young, Cindy & Maulding, Wendy. (1994). Mathematics and Mother Goose. *Teaching Children Mathematics.* 1, (1), 36-38.
  Offers step-by-step ideas for tombining mathematics concepts with literature studies. Although written for teachers of lower grades, many of the ideas are applicable to teaching in other grade levels.

Behavioral Objective Planning Sheet: Chapter 4

AFFECTIVE

Characterization	Behavior is consistent with one's values. Avoid, display, exhibit, internalize, manage, require, resist, resolve, revise
Organization	Hold a commitment to a set of values. Form a reason why one values certain things and not others, make appropriate choices between things that are and are not valued. Abstract, balance, compare, decide, define, formulate, select, systematize, theorize
Valuing	Display behavior consistent with a single belief or attitude in situations where one is neither forced nor asked to comply. Demonstrate a preference or display a high degree of certainty and conviction. Act, argue, convince, debate, display, express, help, organize, prefer
Responding	Comply with given expectations by attending or reacting to certain stimuli. Obey, participate, respond willingly when asked or directed to do something. Applaud, comply, discuss, follow, obey, participate, play, practice, volunteer
Receiving	Be aware of, or passively attend to certain phenomena and stimuli. Listen, be attentive. Attend, beware, control, discern, hear, listen, look, notice, share

PSYCHOMOTOR

Naturalization	Behavior is performed with the least expenditure of energy and comes routine, automatic, spontaneous, and occurs at a high level of proficiency. Automatically, effortlessly, naturally, professionally, routinely, spontaneously, with ease, with perfection, with poise
Articulation	Display coordination of a series of related acts by establishing the appropriate sequence and performing the acts accurately, with control as well as with speed and timing. Confidence, coordination, harmony, integration, proportion, smoothness, speed, stability, timing
Precision	Perform an action independent of either a visual model or a written set of directions. Reproduce the action with control and reduce errors to a minimum. Accurately, errorlessly, independently, proficiently, with control, with balance
Manipulation	Perform selected actions from written or verbal directions without the aid of a visual model or direct observation. Same active verbs as "Imitation" level, but performed from spoken or written (rather than visual) instructions
Imitation	Be exposed to an observable action and overtly imitate it, even at a crude and imperfect level. Align, balance, follow, grasp, hold, place, repeat, rest (on), step (here)

COGNITIVE

Evaluation	Form judgments and make decisions about the value of methods, ideas, people, or products that have a specific purpose. State the bases for these judgments. Appraise, compare, contrast, criticize, defend, judge, justify, support, validate
Synthesis	Produce something unique or original. Solve some unfamiliar problem in a unique way or combine parts to form a unique or novel solution. Categorize, compile, compose, create, design, devise, formulate, predict, produce
Analysis	Identify logical errors (contradiction, erroneous inference) or differentiate among facts, opinions, assumptions, hypotheses, and conclusions. Draw relationships among ideas and compare and contrast. Break down, deduce, diagram, differentiate, distinguish, illustrate, infer, outline, point out, relate, separate out, subdivide
Application	Use previously acquired information in a setting other than the one in which it was learned. Change, compute, demonstrate, develop, modify, operate, organize, prepare, relate, solve, transfer, use
Comprehension	Change the form of a communication; translate; restate what has been read; see connections or relationships among parts of a communication; draw conclusions or see consequences from its information. Convert, defend, discriminate, distinguish, estimate, explain, extend, generalize, infer, paraphrase, predict, summarize
Knowledge	Remember or recall information such as facts, terminology, problem-solving strategies and rules. Define, describe, identify, label, list, match, name, outline, recall, recite, select, state

BRIDGES

KNOWLEDGE — **ACTIVITY**

Chapter 5
Unit and Lesson Planning

Chapter 5	A. Personal, Dialogue, or Buddy Journals	B. Self-Directed Study Activities	C. Cooperative & Collaborative Ideas	D. Whole Class
Introducing the Content	1. Do you **RECALL** a unit of study you liked/disliked? What was your learning like? What do you remember? Was it more/less memorable than other school experiences? Why? 2. What gets your attention in class? What makes your attention drift off?	1. **FIND A PUBLISHED UNIT OF STUDY** for the area in which you'd like to teach. **ANALYZE** it for attention-getting and attention-keeping potential. What changes might you make to enhance its appeal to students? 2. **REVIEW** a unit you've created in the past or one in which you've participated. What attention-getters and other useful devices were employed? What might have enhanced the unit?	1. **DISCUSS IN PAIRS**: What is the most effective way to learn something new? What is the most effective way to **TEACH** something new? Are these the same or different? Why? 2. **BRAINSTORM** several attention-getters for general or specific units of study. Why would each of these be effective?	1. Place ingredients for a cake on the table. **DISCUSS** the idea that in combining ingredients to make a cake, the whole will actually be greater than the sum of the parts. **DRAW THE PARALLEL** that in good unit plans, the result of the whole unit of study is greater than the sum of the separate lessons. If desired, actually **MAKE THE CAKE** and enjoy it as a treat to make the point even more salient!

27

Chapter 5 Continued	A. Personal, Dialogue, or Buddy Journals	B. Self-Directed Study Activities	C. Cooperative & Collaborative Ideas	D. Whole Class
Assimilating /Reviewing the Content	3. Your author suggests that visual devices can be effective for organizing thinking. Have you experienced the use of visual devices recently? How were they helpful/not helpful to you? 4. Do you RECALL experiences with peer or cross-age tutoring? What occurred? What would you change?	3. CREATE A VISUAL DEVICE for this chapter (or for a related reading) which will help you remember key concepts or help you teach with them (pp. 6-7). Share your ideas if you desire. 4. OBSERVE a teacher in a setting where you would like to teach. LIST the schedule s/he follows (including transitions and breaks). If possible, TALK to the teacher and find out how the schedule deviated from her/his plan; and how s/he schedules the day, month, year, etc. ASK if there are particular routines s/he has found helpful over the years.	3. THINK OF A SKILL you could teach. PLAN a fifteen-minute lesson and come prepared next time to TEACH it to a partner or small group. DEBRIEF on your techniques. INCLUDE A VISUAL DEVICE to aid your learners. 4. WORK IN PAIRS to COMPLETE A LESSON PLAN using the GAGNE or HUNTER form (pp. 34-37). Consider including some of the ideas from the ACTIVE LEARNING section of this chapter to add variety to your plan (p. 33). 5. PERUSE a published unit of study in an area of teaching interest. COMPARE the format to the concepts in the Gagne and Hunter plans (pp. 34-37). What do you think?	2. DISPLAY a cartoon on an overhead transparency, such as two dogs looking at a forest while one laments, "So many trees, so little time." Thus it is with teaching: If we try to accomplish each objective separately, we can be overwhelmed and ineffective. Objectives can and must be combined—for our own sanity and to enhance connections students make. 3. As a class, READ the *Reading Teacher* article[1] on group sizes and DISCUSS the ideas of planning for different groups. These group sizes should be considered in lesson planning.

Chapter 5: Checking Your Understanding

Match the following terms with your own definitions or summary statements taken from the text:

System perspective	Unit	Vertical unit planning	Lateral unit planning
Visual device	Programmed instruction	Peer tutoring	Cross-age tutoring
Mastery learning			

True or False:

1. _____ Beginning teachers generally include too much new material in their lessons.

2. _____ It is best to plan evaluative activities like tests and research papers near the middle of a unit so students can see what else they need to learn before the unit ends.

3. _____ It is generally recommended that cross-age tutors be separated from their tutees by 3-4 grade levels.

4. _____ A true system does not exist unless the relationships among parts of the system or unit are planned to connect and build over time.

5. _____ Once determined, criterion levels of behavioral objectives should not be altered.

6. _____ Teachers should organize and sequence curriculum content according to the needs of their students.

7. _____ Teachers should depend primarily upon curriculum guides and textbooks to determine how much content to include in each lesson of a unit.

        1. T   2. F   3. F   4. T   5. F   6. T   7. F

Chapter 5: Performance Assessment Ideas

Individual	Small Group	Whole Class
1. USE the systems idea and MAP (pp. 6-7) a specific system with which you are familiar—include names of schools, communities, etc. as applicable. How does creating the map affect your view of each of the components of the system and their interrelations?	1. WORK with a small group to CREATE some guidelines for peer tutors that a teacher might use to train older students in working with younger peers. You may CONSULT appropriate sources (such as your course text and related professional journal articles) for ideas, but be sure and ACKNOWLEDGE the sources used in your final guidelines. 2. READ the article referenced below[2] and RESPOND to the authors' contention that how a teacher translates a curriculum idea into integrated themes is of utmost importance.	1. OBTAIN a state or district curriculum guide for a local school. As a group, REVIEW the guide for strengths and weaknesses. What recommendations would you make to a state or district curriculum committee for changes to the guide? SUPPORT your recommendations with appropriate source material.

CHILDREN'S LITERATURE CONNECTION

Fleischman, Paul. (1988). *Joyful noise.* **New York: The Trumpet Club. (ISBN 0-440-84078-3)**
This unique book of poetry for two readers gives a different spin to poetry writing and reading. It may give you ideas for other creative ways to use the arts in your units.

Lionni, Leo. (1967). *Frederick.* **New York: Alfred A. Knopf. (ISBN 0-394-82614-0)**
The field mice find that Frederick's poetry helps pass the cold winter days and is, in many ways, as helpful as the food gathered. In like manner, the power of interdisciplinary approaches (bringing the arts and other disciplines together) enhances the learning experiences of our students.

Prelutsky, Jack. (1983). *The Random House book of poetry for children.* **New York: Random House. (ISBN 0-394-85010-6)**
Includes a wide variety of tried and true children pleasers.

Prelutsky, Jack. (1984). *The new kid on the block.* **New York: Scholastic, Inc. (ISBN 0-590-40836-4)**
This collection of poems by a well-known poet can be used to add fun and interest to units of study, or as attention-getters for specific lessons (as discussed in Chapter 6 of your course text).

Webre, Elizabeth C. (1995). Learning about science through poetry. *Teaching K-8.* 50-51.
Summarizes numerous children's literature selections helpful for teaching science through poetry.

REFERENCES

Countryman, Joan. (1993, January). Writing to learn mathematics. *Teaching: K-8.* 51-53.
Describes a number of strategies for connecting writing and mathematics in meaningful ways which can be applied and adapted across grade levels.

Day, Robert. (1994). Learning to navigate the internet. *Teaching Education.* 6, (2), 147-153.
If prospective teachers are going to make the most of available technology in planning and teaching, they may enjoy this easy,m readable introduction to using the internet.

Flynn, Rosalind M. & Carr, Gail A. (1994). Exploring classroom literature through drama: A specialist and a teacher collaborate. *Language Arts.* 71, (1), 38-43.
Describes drama learning strategies applicable to many curriculum areas and pieces of literature. Provides an in-depth look at a 45-minute session with second graders.

Kobrin, Beverly. (1988). *Eyeopeners!* New York: Penguin Books. (ISBN 0-14-046830-7)
Excellent annotated listing of nonfiction resource books to aid interdisciplinary planning.

Kutiper, Karen & Wilson, Patricia. (1993). Updating poetry preferences: A look at the poetry children really like. *The Reading Teacher.* 47, (1), 28-35.
Lists the types of poetry elementary children prefer, provides names of popular poets and collections, and includes recommendations for helping students develop lasting poetry interests.

LaPenta, Marilyn. (1989). *Bulletin board displays.* New York: Macmillan Book Clubs, Inc.
Bulletin boards and other displays related to topics of study should be interesting and interactive. Further, their effectiveness is not necessarily limited to use in elementary schools. This book offers suggestions to get you thinking about how to better utilize bulletin boards in your teaching.

Lehman, Jeffrey R. & Kandl, Thomas M. (1995). Popcorn investigations for integrating mathematics, science, and technology. *School Science and Mathematics.* 95, (1), 46-49.
Suggests several teaching ideas for grades 5-8 using popcorn.

[2]Martin-Kniep, Giselle O.; Feige, Diana Muxworthy; & Soodak, Leslie C. (1995). Curriculum integration: An expanded view of an abused idea. *Journal of Curriculum and Supervision.* 10, (3), 227-249.
Discusses various ways integration can be achieved and emphasizes that curriculum integration also causes some unintentional sacrifice of content, skills, or other aspects.

Max, Ronald W.; Blumenfeld, Phyllis C.; Krajcik, Joseph S.; Blunk, Merrie; Crawford, Barbara; Kelly, Beverly & Meyer, Karen M. (1994). Enacting project-based science: Experiences of four middle grade teachers. *Elementary School Journal.* 94, (5), 517-538.
Presents project-based science as a way to think about innovative instruction. Through four case studies, the authors suggest that teachers need collaboration, practice, and reflection to implement curricular change.

[1]Pardo, Laura S. & Raphael, Taffy E. (1991). Classroom organization for instruction in content areas. *The Reading Teacher.* 44, (8), 556-565.
Notes that use of a variety of grouping strategies in a classroom is not sufficient to create independent and successful learners. Comprehension strategies and other activities must be carefully modeled and utilized in many instructional settings.

Ricklin, Leslie Perfect & Perfect-Miller, Suzanne. (1993, February). A dig that's good enough to eat. *Teaching: K-8*. 50-52.
Describes an integrated lesson plan involving an "archeocake" loaded with "artifacts" from which to teach students about archaeological processes. Creative example of integrating several traditional disciplines and enhancing the inquiry process.

Young, Terrell A. & Vardell, Sylvia. (1993). Weaving Readers Theatre and nonfiction into the curriculum. *The Reading Teacher*. 46, (5), 396-406.
Provides directions for creating readers theatre scripts and performances to enhance students' understanding of nonfiction, content area reading materials.

ACTIVE LEARNING:

ENHANCE your teaching plan in any of the following time-honored ways—or—use the list below to help you brainstorm other interesting activities for students to learn/share something new.

Chain Story: Each student takes a turn telling a portion of the content and stops whenever s/he desires. The next speaker picks up where the previous student left off. **Charades**: Words allowed. **Choral Speaking**: Groups or individuals speak together or in a specific sequence. Several options include: 1. *Refrain: Leader speaks most of the lines and group repeats a refrain.* 2. *Line-a-child or Line-a-group: Each child or group speaks a couplet before the next group takes its turn.* 3. *Antiphonal: Two or more groups of speakers alternate in speaking a piece. Groups may be male and female, high and low pitches, etc., as needed for effect.* 4. *Unison: No subgrouping is used.* 5. *Audience Cue: Cue cards are used to involve the audience as in old-fashioned melodramas or in speaking specific refrains, etc.*	**Improvisation**: No written script. **News Stories**: Reporters report on informational events and key participants. The audience can ask questions, and "experts" may bluff until someone catches them. They can also be restricted to giving only factual and correct answers. **Panel Discussions** or **Debates**: Can be held between important participants of the same time era, differing eras. Can be focused on events and factual information or on the character's motivations, emotions, etc. **Pantomime**: No words, no props (or few props). **Plot Completion**: Students brainstorm what led to the story's beginning and what happened where the story leaves off. **Puppetry**: Stick, Whole Body, Drawings, Paper Bag, Paper Plate, Finger, Shadow, Glove and Sock, Sewn, Mix and Match, Marionettes, Styrofoam Cups, etc.	**Readers' Theater**: Group members read from a script and interact with the audience but not one another. **Storytelling**: Students tell stories in the grand old tradition, emphasizing voice, body, and emotion. **Talk Shows**: Students pose as famous persons, inventors, experts in a particular field, etc., and are interviewed on "television" before a live "studio" audience. **Tape Recording/Radio Shows**: Students record their presentations and can add sound effects, musical backgrounds, etc. **Telephone Conversations**: Held between famous persons being studied, a famous person and a student, etc. **Videotaping**: "Movies," "Commercials," "Film Previews," "Television Shows"

Gagne Lesson Plan Form

1. **Gain Attention:**
   Consider 1) "Opener" questions that amuse, stimulate, bewilder, present an apparent contradiction or inconsistency; and 2) Diagrams, pictures, illustrations, scale models, and films to pique interest.

2. **Inform the Learner(s) of the Objective:**
   What is the behavioral outcome the students are to attain by the end of the lesson? How will it be measured/exhibited?

3. **Stimulate Recall of Prerequisite Learning:**
   Identify and activate key concepts underlying today's lesson.

4. **Present the Stimulus Material:**
   A) Authenticity
   B) Selectivity
   C) Variety (visual, oral, tactile; large group, small group, individual)

5. **Elicit the Desired Behavior:**
   A) Nonevaluative atmosphere (perhaps every-student-response)
   B) Brief
   C) Written, oral, subvocal

6. **Provide Feedback:**
   How will the learner feel affirmed? How will incorrect responses be revised?

7. **Assess the Behavior:**
   (Consider a test, quiz, homework, workbook, performance, lab, oral presentation, extended essay, research paper, independent practice, portfolio entry, etc.)
   A) Immediately, at the end of the lesson
   B) At the end of the week?
   C) At the end of the unit?

Hunter Lesson Plan Form

1. Review:

2. Anticipatory Set:

3. Objectives and Purpose:

4. Input and Modeling:

5. Checking for Understanding:

6. Guided Practice:

7. Closure:

8. Independent Practice:

BRIDGES

KNOWLEDGE — **ACTIVITY**

Chapter 6
Direct Instruction Strategies

Chapter 6	A. Personal, Dialogue, or Buddy Journals	B. Self-Directed Study Activities	C. Cooperative & Collaborative Ideas	D. Whole Class ☺☺☺☺☺☺
Introducing the Content	1. What makes a teacher/class interesting? 2. What makes you want to respond in class? What makes you choose to be silent? Does your participation pattern vary among classes? Why?	1. WATCH someone do a "direct instruction" lesson. What strengths or weaknesses do you note in the approach?	1. BRAINSTORM meanings for the terms "homework" and "busywork." How are the two similar? How are they different? What are the goals of each? **CREATE A CHART** (pp. 6-7) that compares/contrasts your ideas. You may want to differentiate between "ideal" and "less than ideal" uses of each.	1. Use a **COVERT RESPONSE TECHNIQUE** (p. 14) in today's lecture, perhaps with all or part of the chapter practice questions. **DISCUSS** how it feels to be able to respond "safely" as opposed to being "put on the spot" in class.

38

Chapter 6 Continued	A. Personal, Dialogue, or Buddy Journals	B. Self-Directed Study Activities	C. Cooperative & Collaborative Ideas	D. Whole Class
Assimilating /Reviewing the Content	3. What comes to mind when you hear the word busywork? How about the word homework? How are the two similar? How are they different? What are the goals of each? 4. How do you feel about grading work at the beginning of class. How many of your teachers did that? Does your experience match the 50% quoted in Chapter 6?	2. Think about the idea that "teaching is not telling." How do you reconcile that idea with the concept of direct instruction?	2. **LIST** the 7 steps of lesson planning according to Gagne or Hunter. **CREATE A GRAPHIC** to show the direct instruction options for addressing each and **SHARE** with the class. 3. **ROLE PLAY** types of student responses and **CHART** ways to deal with them.	2. Return to the **BEHAVIORAL OBJECTIVE PLANNING SHEET** (p. 26) and **DRAW** in a line to divide each **OVAL** into Type 1 and Type 2 behaviors. **EXPLAIN** that Chapter 6 focuses on supporting Type 1 behaviors, and Chapter 7 focuses on Type 2 behaviors. As a class, **NOTE** the meaning of Type 1 and Type 2 behaviors somewhere on the planning sheet.

Chapter 6: Checking Your Understanding

True or False:

1. _____ Independent practice should help students internalize a behavior or response so that it becomes automatic.
2. _____ It is important to give highly specific feedback to students as they practice a new skill or behavior so they can avoid any errors.
3. _____ Direct instruction is most efficient for teaching Type 2 learning outcomes such as facts, rules, and action sequences.
4. _____ A good way to determine when to reteach a concept to the whole class is to see how many high and low performers made errors on the practice assignment.
5. _____ A teacher should determine what type of feedback to offer a student based on the correctness and surety of the student's response.
6. _____ Information taught in a direct instruction format is most easily tested through multiple choice, listing, matching, and fill-in exercises.
7. _____ Teachers should use the most powerful prompt possible to help learners perform, even if a less intrusive prompt may work.
8. _____ Programmed instruction, computer-assisted instruction, peer and cross-age tutoring, and some audiolingual approaches can also be used for direct instruction.

Multiple Choice:

9. _____ Which of the following are the most common strategies for dealing with incorrect student responses? (Mark all that apply)
   a. Ask student to repeat the correct response after you model it
   b. Review key facts or rules required to achieve the solution
   c. Ask students to recite by memory the steps required to solve a problem
   d. Offer prompts or hints representing a partially correct answer
   e. Use another problem and guide the student to the correct answer

   1. T   2. F   3. F   4. T   5. T   6. T   7. F   8. T   9. b, d, e

Chapter 6: Performance Assessment Ideas

Individual	Small Group	Whole Class
1. **OBTAIN** a curriculum guide for an area in which you'd like to teach. **CHOOSE** a subject area and **PLAN A LESSON** you believe would best be accomplished through direct instruction. Include your lesson plan and your reflections on the process in your portfolio. 2. **OBSERVE** a lesson using the direct instruction method. **CRITIQUE** it from your understanding of direct instruction. Place your observation notes and critique in your portfolio.	1. **CHOOSE** several articles from those referenced in this chapter (either in the text or in this guide). Have each group member **READ** a different article (see **REFERENCES**, (p. 42) and **PREPARE A BRIEF SUMMARY** of how its content applies to the idea of direct instruction as you understand it. Have each group member **WRITE A 1-2 SENTENCE CRITIQUE** of the article's importance and the group member's delivery. Include a copy of the article, the summary, and the group critiques in your portfolio.	1. **CHOOSE** a lesson from this course (or another lesson all class members can experience, such as one on a videotape) and **EVALUATE** it for for Type 1 and Type 2 behaviors. What do you notice about the lesson and the behaviors required? What would you change?

CHILDREN'S LITERATURE CONNECTION

Willis, Jeanne. (1988). *Earthlets as explained by Professor Xargle.* New York: E.P. Dutton. (ISBN 0-525-44465-3)
Professor Xargle uses direct instruction and is anything but boring. He combines direct instruction with a field trip, once he has built important background. (This book can also be used to review Chapter 5 content and emphasize the importance of perspective. Questions such as, "How do we look to Xargle's people?" "How do we look as teachers?" "How do our units look to students?" can help us "step back" and look at our planning from varied perspectives.)

Brown, Margaret Wise. (1949). *The important book.* New York: HarperCollins Children's Books; New York: HarperCollins Publishers, 1990.
The predictable format of this book, "The important thing about_____ is that_____" lends itself to a number of reading/writing/sharing activities wherein students assign perspective and value to ideas.

REFERENCES

Barton, James. (1995, May). Revitalize classroom discussions. *Education Digest.* 48-52.
Summarizes several ways to make instruction more effective through good discussion.

Berghoff, Beth & Egawa, Kathryn. (1991). No more "rocks": Grouping to give students control of their learning. *The Reading Teacher.* 44, (8), 536-541.
Discusses pros and cons of traditional grouping methods and includes a helpful chart for expanding group assignment to include independent, paired, small group and whole group instruction.

Chambers, Donald L. (1995). Improving instruction by listening to children. *Teaching Children Mathematics.* 1, (6), 378-380.
Suggests that teachers need to attend more to students' responses and thinking. Gives examples of how classroom dialogue where teachers listen well.

Hadaway, Nancy L, & Young, Terrell A. (1994). Content literacy and language learning: Instructional decisions. *The Reading Teacher.* 47, (7), 522-527.
Describes ways teachers can model the use of comprehension strategies for their students. Includes a number of teaching ideas and activities.

Keegan, Suzi & Shrake, Karen. (1991). Literature study groups: An alternative to ability grouping. *The Reading Teacher.* 44, (8), 542-547.
Describes how to implement, conduct, and evaluate literature study groups as an alternative to traditional ability grouping. The idea can be extended beyond reading of novels to reading of various texts in other disciplines.

Moss, Barbara. (1995). Using children's nonfiction tradebooks as read-alouds. *Language Arts.* 72, (2), 122-126.
Offers reasons for reading nonfiction aloud and provides steps for planning nonfiction read-aloud experiences.

Naughton, Victoria M. (1993/1994). Creative mapping for content reading. *Journal of Reading.* 37, (4), 324-326.
Describes creative mapping as a pictorial version of semantic mapping as a tool to help students better understand content materials. Includes a description of how to model the process and a sample map.

Olson, Mary W. & Gee, Thomas C. (1991). Content reading instruction in the primary grades: Perceptions and strategies. *The Reading Teacher.* 45, (4), 298-307.
Discusses the importance of helping young children develop skill in reading informational texts. Describes six strategies for helping students develop greater content reading proficiency.

Spiegel, Dixie Lee. (1992). Blending whole language and systematic direct instruction. *The Reading Teacher.* 46, (1), 38-44.
Summarizes what she believes to be the contributions of the whole language movement as well as the advantages of systematic direct instruction. Suggests that while many view the two as mutually exclusive or conflicting, bridges can and should be built by educators to take advantage of the strengths in both instructional approaches.

BRIDGES

KNOWLEDGE — **ACTIVITY**

Chapter 7
Indirect Instruction Strategies

Chapter 7	A. *Personal, Dialogue, or Buddy Journals*	B. *Self-Directed Study Activities*	C. *Cooperative & Collaborative Ideas*	D. *Whole Class* ☺☺☺☺☺☺
Introducing the Content	1. Do you have any memories of the "scientific method"? Are they positive? Why or why not? When did you use it? 2. Do you remember any "real discussions" in a class? What made them work? What makes some discussions fail?	1. COMPARE/CONTRAST the idea of direct versus indirect instruction. What do you see as the advantages/drawbacks of each? With which are you more familiar?	1. If you have met in the same group throughout this course, MEET with that group to DISCUSS how it has functioned. COMPARE your learning and experiences in the group activities with whole class and individual activities. What do you find? Do others in your group agree with you?* 2. COMPARE the DIRECT INSTRUCTION LESSON PLAN (pp. 48-49) with the GAGNE and HUNTER LESSON FORMS (pp. 34-37). What do you notice?	1. CREATE and DISPLAY an overhead transparency of workers building a building or some other type of construction. DRAW A PARALLEL with constructivist thought wherein learners construct personal meaning from their interactions with their environments. BRAINSTORM the implications of a learner's environment in such a view (i.e., early experiences and the nature of social interactions will be pivotal, etc.)

*(If you haven't met with the same people, meet in a group to discuss your group experiences in more general terms or to discuss how group work may have altered your experience.)

Chapter 7 Continued	A. Personal, Dialogue, or Buddy Journals	B. Self-Directed Study Activities	C. Cooperative & Collaborative Ideas	D. Whole Class
Assimilating /Reviewing the Content	3. What does discovery learning mean to you? How does it **COMPARE** to the idea of inquiry learning or problem-solving curricula? 4. Have you ever experienced a student-centered approach to teaching which resulted in "pooled ignorance" (where the teacher failed to guide the instruction sufficiently)? **HOW DID YOU FEEL** about the experience? What role might curriculum guidelines play in helping teachers avoid such events?	2. **MAKE A VISUAL** which captures the content of Chapters 6 and 7 for you as a future teacher. 3. How would you **DEFINE** "social framing"? What **IMPLICATIONS** do you see for this concept in the setting where you hope to teach? 4. **READ** one or more articles on discussion referenced on pages 46-47. **WRITE** and **SHARE A RESPONSE** to the information.	3. **CREATE A VISUAL** for the roles of a teacher in indirect and direct settings.[1,2] **SHARE** your visual with the class. 4. With a partner, **THINK** of an example of direct/indirect instruction used in this course (or in another). Was it a good choice for the topic and the objective? Why or why not? 5. **ROLE PLAY** questioning using the search and discovery process. Use the **TALKING CHIPS** (p. 47) activity to encourage each group member to fully participate in the discussion.	2. **INTRODUCE** the idea of **PARAPHRASE PASSPORT** (p. 47) before the class discussion today. At the conclusion of the lesson, **REFLECT** on the success of the strategy in enhancing discussion.

Chapter 7: Checking Your Understanding

Multiple Choice:

1. According to constructivist theories, indirect instruction is important because knowledge results:
   a. by forming rules and hypotheses about "reality" from one's own perspective
   b. from being exposed to the facts about the world as interpreted by others
   c. from careful, systematic memorization on one's personal timetable
   d. from students "telling" other students about the world

2. Deductive reasoning skills are helpful for students because: (Mark all that apply)
   a. much information can be obtained by beginning with a theory and testing or experimenting with it to see how accurately it predicts events
   b. generalizations can be misleading if they are not carefully tested
   c. knowing that something generally occurs can alert us to watch for similar situations and act accordingly
   d. what occurs in one place is bound to occur in another

3. Which of the following strategies are included in indirect instruction?
   a. cooperative learning and programmed instruction
   b. self-directed inquiry and cooperative learning
   c. inquiry learning and memorization
   d. discovery learning and step-by-step procedures

4. A helpful way to think about and plan for constructivist approaches to learning is to present curriculum in:
   a. a step-by-step, logical sequence
   b. a pre-structured unit of study
   c. a problem-solving format
   d. an open discussion or demonstration format

True or False:

5. _____ Deductive reasoning generally leads to greater levels of complexity because patterns and generalizations are accepted as fact.
6. _____ Students can be aided in taking responsibility for their own learning through opportunities to engage in self-evaluation.
7. _____ Indirect instruction is more complex than direct instruction with regard to teacher behavior, but not student behavior.
8. _____ A single, good question is the centerpiece of indirect instruction.
9. _____ Student dialogue plays an important part in the process of indirect instruction.
10. _____ Teachers should avoid sharing their personal feelings and experiences related to a specific lesson.

1. a   2. a, b, c   3. b   4. c   5. F   6. T   7. F   8. F   9. T   10. F

Chapter 7: Performance Assessment Ideas		
Individual	*Small Group*	*Whole Class*
1. **REFLECT** on your own experiences with cooperative/collaborative learning either in this course or in another setting. How did the experiences **COMPARE** to the information in this chapter? What questions do you have about the processes? What plans do you have for using such strategies in your own teaching? Why do you feel this way?	1. **BRAINSTORM** two or three teaching situations for which a cooperative/collaborative approach would be appropriate. **WRITE** a short vignette for each, along with how you envision the strategy working. **PRESENT** your ideas to the class and revise where needed. **TEST** your ideas if there is an available setting.	1. **PERUSE** cooperative learning manuals and books and select 2-3 team-building activities for the class. **PARTICIPATE** in the activities and **DEBRIEF** regarding their effectiveness in helping you feel a part of the group. **BRAINSTORM** other ideas about what helps you feel included in a group and **COMPILE** a class list.

CHILDREN'S LITERATURE CONNECTION

Slepian, Jan & Seidler, Ann. (1967). *The hungry thing.* New York: Scholastic. (ISBN 0-590-09179-4)
Just as the young boy aids the town by figuring out the pattern in the Thing's communication, so our students are engaged in and aided in their learning by being allowed to "discover" and "figure out" patterns in the content we study and share together. [There is also a second book by the same authors, **The hungry thing returns.** *(1990). New York: Scholastic, Inc. (ISBN 0-590-42891-8).]*

REFERENCES

Aker, Don. (1992). From runned to ran: One journey toward a critical literacy. *Journal of Reading.* **36, (2), 104-112.**
Describes his evolving understanding as he gained a more constructivist view of reading. Can be helping in helping to clarify differences between traditional views of reading comprehension and constructivist views of students creating their own meanings.

Barton, James. (1995). Conducting effective classroom discussion. *Journal of Reading.* **38, (5), 346-350.**
Discusses the complexity of leading successful discussions and offers specific strategies for enhancing class discussions.

Bertheau, Myrna. (1994). The most important thing is . . . . *Teaching Children Mathematics.* **92), 112-115.**
Describes how a teacher follows the children's lead to integrate literature and curriculum in discovery learning about shapes. A useful example of how teachers can build on student interests to develop integrated curriculum lessons. (Refers to **The Important Book,** *see* **Children's Literature Connection,** *Chapter 6, p. 41).*

[2]Eeds, Maryann & Peterson, Ralph. (1991). Teacher as curator: Learning to talk about literature. *The Reading Teacher.* 45, (2), 118-126.
Suggests that teachers think of reading as a transaction between a reader and a text, and consider their own role in the reading process from new vantage points. Includes excerpts from student discussions and illustrates ways to interact with students.

Kamii, Constance & Lewis, Barbara. (1993, January). The harmful effects of algorithms . . . in primary arithmetic. *Teaching: K-8.* 36-38.
Helps elucidate a constructivist view of learning by explaining how children must create a personal understanding of math concepts rather than memorize one.

[1]O'Flahavan, John F. (1994/1995). Teacher role options in peer discussions about literature. *The Reading Teacher.* 48, (4), 354-356.
Suggests an outline for a 30-minute session including discussion about a particular text. Suggests that teachers adopt the role best fitting the needs of a particular group, choosing from coaching, scaffolding, or combining both.

Swift, Kathleen. (1993). Try Reading Workshop in your classroom. *The Reading Teacher.* 46, (5), 366-371.
A sixth-grade teacher discusses her experiences in implementing a Reading Workshop in her classroom.

ACTIVE LEARNING

TALKING CHIPS is a cooperative learning activity designed to encourage participation by each group member. It proceeds in the following manner:
1. Pose a question for which there is not a clear, literal answer.
2. Give each member in the group a stack of colored papers or chips (each member receives a different color).
3. Have groups discuss the question, each member placing a chip in a center pile whenever s/he speaks.
4. Have groups respond to the question as a class, summarizing their group's ideas.
5. Have students compare their chip piles. Ideal piles should include a fairly balanced grouping of chips.

Kagan, Spencer. (1990). *Cooperative learning resources for teachers.* San Juan Capistrano, CA: Printing and Reprographics—University of California, Riverside.

Templeton, S. (1991). *Teaching the integrated language arts.* Boston: Houghton Mifflin, 107-109.

PARAPHRASE PASSPORT is another cooperative learning activity to encourage better discussions. After someone has contributed an idea to the group discussion, another person must correctly restate that idea before contributing his or her own idea.

Direct Instruction Lesson Plan

1. **Daily Review and Checking Previous Day's Work:**

2. **Presenting and Structuring:**
   Part-to-whole, sequential, combinatorial, comparative; rule-example-rule

3. **Guided Student Practice:**
   Nonevaluative-covert; feedback prompt, wrong answer conversion plans

4. **Feedback and Correctives:**

5. **Independent Practice:**
   A) Let students know the reason for doing the practice
   B) Brief, nonevaluative, supportive
   C) Ensure success
   D) Receive feedback (how will students receive it?)
   E) Progress, challenge, variety planned for

6. **Weekly and Monthly Reviews:**

BRIDGES

KNOWLEDGE — **ACTIVITY**

Chapter 8
Questioning Strategies

Chapter 8	A. Personal, Dialogue, or Buddy Journals	B. Self-Directed Study Activities	C. Cooperative & Collaborative Ideas	D. Whole Class ☺☺☺☺☺☺
Introducing the Content	1. Could a question be used as a punishment? As a reward? Have you ever **EXPERIENCED** either? What do you recall?	1. Does asking questions really enhance learning? Why do you **FEEL** this way? 2. Try reading this chapter using the **SQ3R** technique (p. 54) and asking yourself questions. What did you notice about your experience?	1. **THINK BACK** to the **WRITTEN CONVERSATION** activity on the first day of class (pp. viii-ix). What did you learn about asking questions from hearing others share their information? **DO** the activity again in small groups and **ASK "BETTER" QUESTIONS** this time. What implications do you see from this experience for improving your ability to pose helpful questions to your future students?	1. Introduce and do the **MODIFIED REQUEST** procedure (p. 54) for this chapter and an upcoming test in the course. 2. **COMPLETE** a "pop quiz" like **"HOW IT WORKS"** (p. 57). **DISCUSS** how most students answered each question correctly, in spite of limited comprehension of the piece. **LEAD** into a discussion of assessment issues, especially those of traditional assessment.

Chapter 8 Continued	A. Personal, Dialogue, or Buddy Journals	B. Self-Directed Study Activities	C. Cooperative & Collaborative Ideas	D. Whole Class
Assimilating /Reviewing the Content	2. In your experience, how long do teachers generally wait for students to respond to their questions? How long should they wait? Why? 3. THINK BACK to ways teachers determined who to call on in school. What patterns did you like? Dislike? Why?	3. CONSIDER the idea of cultural wait times for questions and answers. What feels comfortable to you in a conversational setting? In an academic setting? SURVEY several peers and see if you find any differences among them. 4. READ the information on QARS (pp. 55-56). How might you APPLY this information to your teaching goals? To your personal learning strategies?	2. BRAINSTORM all the reasons teachers ask questions. CATEGORIZE your responses and then COMPARE them to those in your text. Did you think of any your author didn't? 3. DISCUSS the following questions in pairs or small groups: Do convergent and divergent questions have right/wrong answers? Why or why not? 4. IMPROVISE a classroom scene ROLE PLAY a teacher asking probes to help a student extend his or her thinking. SHARE your improvisation with the class and DEBRIEF on the way your "instructor" responded to the student.	3. ASK the class the following questions and LIST their responses on the chalkboard: What is a question? When is it effective? 4. USE DIFFERENT LENGTHS OF WAIT TIME throughout the lesson today. DRAW ATTENTION to these variations and DEBRIEF. 5. BRAINSTORM teacher behaviors that defeat the power of questioning. LIST responses on the chalkboard to lead into a discussion of the topic. 6. DEBATE the following topic: Teachers should require all students to participate in answering questions in class.

Chapter 8: Checking Your Understanding

Match the following terms with your own definitions or summary statements taken from the text:

Analysis question	Comprehension question	Evaluation question	Synthesis question
Type 1 behaviors	Application question	Probe	Type 2 behaviors
Knowledge question

True or False:

1._____According to Rowe, there are two kinds of wait time—the time a learner is given to respond to a question, and the time after a learner's response until the teacher speaks.
2._____Questions should encourage students to think about and act upon the material you have structured and presented.
3._____Divergent questions have more than one response, because all responses to them are correct.
4._____60-70% of all school time is devoted to questions and answers.
5._____Teachers often reward an answer to a question when it is one they expect.
6._____One reason higher level questioning in classrooms may not appear to influence student achievement is that student achievement is often measured using standardized tests which often test for lower level, recall knowledge.
7._____Teachers should respond to questions and answers as quickly as possible to keep the flow of the class moving.
8._____Most questions teachers ask of students require only simple recall of facts.

	1. T	2. T	3. F	4. F	5. T	6. T	7. F	8. T

Chapter 8: Performance Assessment Ideas		
Individual	*Small Group*	*Whole Class*
1. WRITE a brief, reflective piece on what you have learned about preparing for tests. What do you look for in order to predict what will be on a teacher's first test? How do you prepare for subsequent tests? How do you prepare for different kinds of test questions? Do you prefer to study alone or in groups? Why? How does your test experience inform you as a future teacher?	1. In your group, BRAINSTORM a set of questions for this chapter and MAKE A TEST for the class. SCORE the "tests" and then CRITIQUE the questions. You might use a code on the test to indicate the group source for the question to facilitate feedback and understanding afterward. What did you learn about your test-writing skills? What would you do differently next time?	1. READ the chapter and WRITE at least two questions you could ask in class. Come to class with the questions, and try to ASK at least one of them. At the end of the discussion/lecture, COMPARE the questions each person brought. What do you notice about the questions? Was it helpful to come to class with specific questions in mind? Why or why not?

CHILDREN'S LITERATURE CONNECTION

Steig, William. (1984). CDC? Canada: HarperCollins Canada Ltd. (ISBN 0-374-41024-0)
Share some of the pages of this book with students using overhead transparencies. As they figure out the meanings, ask them to share their level of involvement and satisfaction in answering the question of what each page meant.

REFERENCES

Baloche, Lynda. (1994). Breaking down the walls. Integrating creative questioning and cooperative learning into the social studies. *The Social Studies.* **85, (1), 25-30.**
Offers suggestions on how to ask questions using specific strategies. Illustrates with actual classroom dialogue and examples.

Gilles, Carol; Dickinson, Jean, McBride, Cheryl, & Vandover, Marc. (1994). Discussing our questions and questioning our discussions: Growing into literature study. *Language Arts.* **71, (7), 499-508.**
Notes that getting "grand conversations" going in classrooms takes persistence, reflection, and adaptability. Shares stories of three teachers' efforts to encourage student discussion.

Gillespie, Cindy. (1990). Questions about student-generated questions. *Journal of Reading.* 34, (4), 250-257.
Discusses the value of helping students generate their own questions for reading and offers strategies for teaching them to do so.

Manzo, Anthony V. & Manzo, Ula Casale. (1990). Note Cue: A comprehension and participation training strategy. *Journal of Reading.* 33, (8), 608-611.
Details a structured approach for helping students learn to ask and answer questions and comment in class in more successful ways. The authors suggest that the strategy is especially well-studied for ESL, at-risk, and culturally different students.

ACTIVE LEARNING

SQ3R is a mnemonic first suggested as an aid for college students in studying their texts. The process follows five steps:
1. **Survey**: Students look over the material to be read, think about headings, glance at figures and graphs, etc. to determine the main idea of the passage.
2. **Question**: Students turn each section heading into a question they seek to answer as they read.
3. **Read**: Students read the passage, seeking to answer their questions.
4. **Recite**: Students review periodically during their reading by reciting questions and answers in their heads. This helps them maintain focus and check for understanding.
5. **Review**: Students attempt to answer their questions without looking back at the text. They then refer to the text where needed.

MODIFIED REQUEST is a cooperative learning procedure designed to encourage students to ask their own questions and direct their own learning. The procedure is outlined below:
1. Tell students the topic of the day.
2. Give students 1-2 minutes to write questions about it.
3. Have students ask you questions about the topic.
4. Answer each question fully. Pose no questions yourself.
5. Invite students to ask more questions.

Kagan, Spencer. (1990). *Cooperative learning resources for teachers.* San Juan Capistrano, CA: Printing and Reprographics—University of California, Riverside.

QARS (QUESTION-ANSWER-RELATIONSHIPS) is a helpful mnemonic for teaching students how to better comprehend what they read. Students learn that answers to questions come from different sources: the text and their own experiences. Raphael (1986) calls these "In the Book" and "In My Head". Within each category are two subcategories.

For the "In the Book" category, the answer may be: a) stated explicitly in the text, within a single sentence of text; or b) available from the text but require the reader to put together information from different sentences to determine it. The former is called "Right There". The latter can be called either "Think and Search" or "Putting It Together".

The "In My Head" category can also be divided into two types, once students have a clear understanding that their background knowledge is a relevant source of information for answering questions. The two categories are: a) "Author and You"; and b) "On My Own". The 2 figures on pages 55 and 56 help illustrate these relationships:

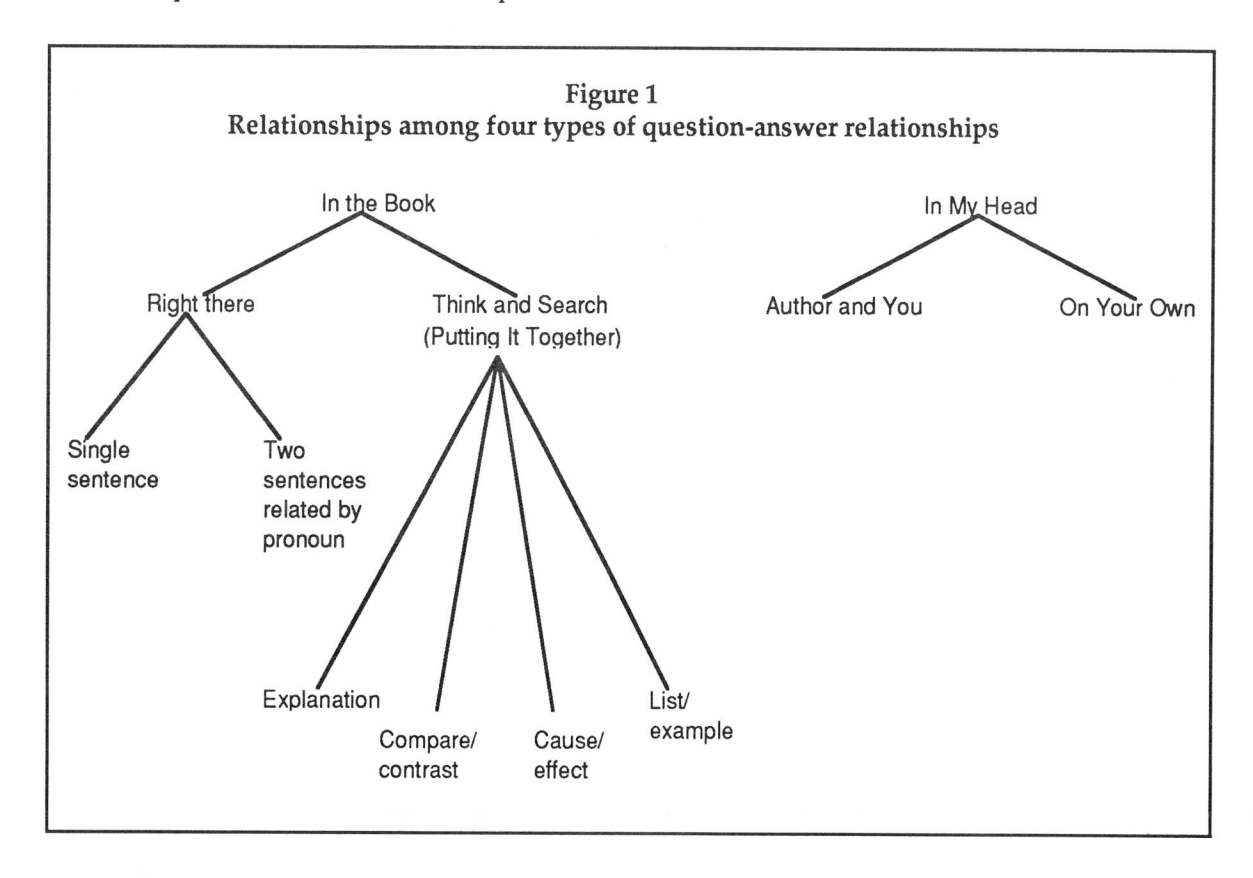

Figure 1
Relationships among four types of question-answer relationships

In the Book
- Right there
  - Single sentence
  - Two sentences related by pronoun
- Think and Search (Putting It Together)
  - Explanation
  - Compare/contrast
  - Cause/effect
  - List/example

In My Head
- Author and You
- On Your Own

Figure 2
Illustrations to explain QARs to students

In the Book QARS

Right There
The answer is in the text, usually easy to find. The words used to make up the question and words used to answer the question are Right There in the same sentence.

| One day there was . . .

 So, Jack rode a horse to school today! | What did Jack ride to school today?

 (a horse) |

Think and Search
(Putting It Together)
The answer is in the story, but you need to put together different story parts to find it. Words for the question and words for the answer are not found in the same sentence. They come from different parts of the text.

| First, you get some bread.

 Second, you get a knife.

 Third, you get the peanut butter. | How do you make a peanut butter sandwich? |

In My Head QARs

Author and You
The answer is not in the story. You need to think about what you already know, what the author tells you in the text, and how it fits together.

| One day there was . . . | |

On My Own
The answer is not in the story. You can even answer the question without reading the story. You need to use your own experience.

Raphael, Taffy. (1986). Teaching question answer relationships revisited. *The Reading Teacher*. 516-522.

How It Works (Radio Passage)

The scope calibrator is basically a simple solid-state astable multivibrator designed to close tolerances. Transistors Q2 and Q3 comprise the multivibrator, whose frequency is determined essentially by the values of the timing components C1, C2, R3 and R4. The nominal 1020-Hz frequency can be reduced to an exact 1000-Hz signal by merely shunting C1 and C2 with a 20-pf. capacitor.

Emitter follower Q4 serves to isolate the multivibrator from the load effects of the output circuit while functioning as an impedence-matching device. Transistor Q1 serves only as a battery condition indicator. It is employed in an emitter follower configuration with a 10-volt lamp (I1) serving both as an indicator and as the emitter resistor.

As the source battery deteriorates, its output gradually approaches the zener (d1) voltage, reducing Q1's base bias and thus causing the lamp to glow more and more dimly. This can be observed by pressing the battery test switch (S2). However, because the calibrator would normally be used only on occasion rather than continuously, the life of the battery can be expected to approach its no-use shelf-life.

1. The scope calibrator is designed to
   a. receive radio messages
   b. close tolerances
   c. transmit radar signals

2. The frequency of the multivibrator is determined essentially by
   a. the values of the timing components
   b. the number of times the calibrator is used
   c. the condition of the battery indicator

3. The frequency of the multivibrator can be reduced to an exact 1000-Hz signal by
   a. redirecting the voltage of the emitter follower
   b. shunting C1 and C2 with a 20-pf. capacitor
   c. avoiding the deterioration of the battery

4. Transistor Q1 serves only as
   a. a reciprocal multivibrator
   b. a signal reflector
   c. a battery condition indicator

5. As the source battery deteriorates,
   a. the lamp glows more and more dimly
   b. the battery switch reverses its primary polarity
   c. the emitter follower is replaced by the emitter resistor

6. The life of the battery can be expected to approach shelf-life because
   a. the calibrator draws very little voltage
   b. the calibrator would normally be used occasionally
   c. the calibrator operates on low amperage

BRIDGES

Chapter 9
Self-Directed Learning

KNOWLEDGE — **ACTIVITY**

Chapter 9	A. Personal, Dialogue, or Buddy Journals	B. Self-Directed Study Activities	C. Cooperative & Collaborative Ideas	D. Whole Class ☺☺☺☺☺☺
Introducing the Content	1. Are you a self-starter? Does this ability/way of being vary in your life (e.g., you're a self-starter in art, but not in math, etc.)? 2. How do you feel when teachers open up study options in a particular course?	1. SURVEY your friends and/or neighbors regarding their study/learning strategies. What did you discover? Don't forget to INCLUDE YOUR OWN APPROACHES in your research. 2. What does the term "motivation" mean to you? How is motivation related to intrinsic and extrinsic rewards? Can you "motivate" another? PERUSE an article on motivation (see **References** for this chapter, p. 62) or one you find yourself. Does the information alter any of your views? How?	1. Work with a partner to COMPLETE THE STUDY GUIDE (p. 66) for this chapter.[1] DEBRIEF on whether the guide was useful to you as a learner.	1. MODEL RECIPROCAL TEACHING (pp. 62-64) with a passage. DISCUSS the gradual release of responsibility involved in this approach. DEBRIEF pros and cons of the approach.

Chapter 9 Continued	A. Personal, Dialogue, or Buddy Journals	B. Self-Directed Study Activities	C. Cooperative & Collaborative Ideas	D. Whole Class
Assimilating /Reviewing the Content	3. How do you "learn" best? Is that the same as how you "study" best? 4. How did you arrive at your current learning/studying strategies? Are there any which you feel need revision?	3. MAP key ideas (pp. 6-7) of the chapter or MAKE A SET OF NOTES you think would help you or your peers recall information in this chapter. REFLECT on the process you used: What did you do and how did it work?	2. Work with a partner or small group to CREATE A SIMPLE GRAPHIC, POEM, OR SONG SUMMARIZING KEY CONCEPTS in this chapter and present it to the class (p. 65). 4. SHARE a favorite/useful study strategy with your group.	2. Ask students to EXPLAIN, from a constructivist view, how an independent learner is developed. DISCUSS the role of speech in learning at an interpersonal and intrapersonal level. 3. BRAINSTORM dialogue patterns that have occurred in class. Why is dialogue so important? STRESS the idea that it's hard to develop your own voice and make decisions if you don't trust in yourself, if you only learn to "parrot" the teacher, if you are not allowed to speak, etc.

Chapter 9: Checking Your Understanding

Multiple Choice:

1. To successfully demonstrate mental procedures, teachers should: (Mark all that apply)
   a. focus the learner's attention on the skill to be learned
   b. speak in educational terms when demonstrating so students hear and can use the proper academic terms
   c. combine steps of the process to simplify ideas
   d. work to make demonstrations particularly memorable in some way

2. Inner speech does *not* help learners:
   a. guide their actions
   b. think about their thinking
   c. internalize ideas from their experiences
   d. maintain dependence upon teacher prompts

3. A good way for teachers to enhance self-directed learning among culturally diverse students is:
   a. involve students in dialogues with one another and the teacher in addition to explaining and lecturing
   b. present important material in a clear, direct instruction format
   c. respond quickly to any student error with evaluative information to correct the problem
   d. group students according to similar backgrounds and lecture to their needs

True or False:

4. _____The reason cognitive learning strategies are so important is because they provide specific ways for students to learn and remember specific content: They offer a carefully tailored approach for learning special subjects.
5. _____In mental modeling a teacher demonstrates verbally the reasoning s/he used to solve a particular problem to help students apply similar reasoning in their own thinking.
6. _____A good teaching strategy for helping students learn to think is to ask students to share how they arrived at a particular concept or solution to a problem.
7. _____There are general approaches for solving problems, (such as IDEAL), that can be taught to students to aid them in solving problems in a number of disciplines or subject areas.

    1. a, d   2. d   3. a   4. F   5. T   6. T   7. T

Chapter 9: Performance Assessment Ideas

Individual	Small Group	Whole Class
1. **READ** all or part of Chapter 9 and **PAY CLOSE ATTENTION TO YOUR MENTAL PROCESSES**. What kinds of things do you notice yourself doing before you read? During? After? **WRITE** a short reflection on what you discovered. 2. **CHOOSE A TEXT** you will be studying (or teaching) and **CREATE A STUDY GUIDE** for one of the chapters or sections. What did you discover as you worked on the guide?	1. **CHOOSE A SHORT PASSAGE** from a professional journal, newspaper, magazine, etc. **READ** it and determine where a younger reader might have difficulty understanding the message. **SHARE** the passage with a small group and **"TALK THROUGH"** how you make sense of the passage, especially those areas where you feel a student might have difficulty. What do you see as the value of "mental modeling" in this activity? How might this insight apply to you as a future teacher? 2. **READ** the article[2] referenced below. **DIFFERENTIATE** between teacher hearing and teacher listening. What implications does this piece have for helping students feel greater motivation and academic success? What differences do you see between listening **to** and listening **for**?	1. **LISTEN** as the course instructor models a particular learning strategy. **THINK** about what you are hearing and how this modeling helps or doesn't help you as a learner. What insights do you have? **WRITE** a short reflection about your thinking.

CHILDREN'S LITERATURE CONNECTION

Hoffman, Mary. (1991). *Amazing Grace.* **New York: Penguin Books. (ISBN 0-8037-1040-2)**
With wise guidance, Grace capitalizes on her natural abilities. The same is true for students with whom we work—much of what we consider "motivation" involves coming to know students and offer opportunities for scholastic experiences to build upon their personal knowledge and interests.

REFERENCES

[2]Davis, Brent A. (1994). Mathematics teaching: Moving from telling to listening. *Journal of Curriculum and Supervision.* 9, (3), 267-2283.
Contrasts two teaching approaches to mathematics and notes the importance of how teachers listen to students. Reminds the reader that listening differs from hearing.

Davis, Susan J. (1994, October). Make reading rewarding, NOT rewarded. *Education Digest.* 63-65.
Notes that real reasons for reading are better motivators than extrinsic rewards.

Ediger, Marlow. (1994, Fall). Pupils learn on their own in science. *Science Activities.* 31, (3), 15-16.
Discusses ways teachers can set up an environment which encourages effective incidental learning of science concepts.

Greenwood, Scott C. (1995). Learning contracts and transaction: A natural marriage in the middle. *Language Arts.* 72, (2), 88-96.
Suggests that using learning contracts with middle school students can help build community as it builds language arts skill.

Klem, John. (No date). *Motivating the unmotivated.* Phi Delta Kappa Educational Foundation Workshop Manual. Bloomington, Indiana: Phi Delta Kappa.
In this compilation of handouts from motivation seminar (presented across the nation), Klem hits on several points relating to student motivation which directly affect management issues.

Menke, Deborah J. & Pressley, Michael. (1994). Elaborative interrogation: Using "why" questions to enhance the learning from text. *Journal of Reading.* 37, (8), 642-645.
Note that students' factual memory is greatly improved when students are taught to respond to factual statements in text with "why" questions, (e.g., "Why does the seal live with a group of other seals?").

[1]Miller, Kathleen K. & George, John E. (1992). Expository Passage Organizers: Models for reading and writing. *Journal of Reading.* 35, (5), 372-377.
Offers a sample Expository Passage Organizer and explains how it can help students in their study.

Oldfather, Penny. (1995). Commentary: What's needed to maintain and extend motivation for literacy in the middle grades. *Journal of Reading.* 38, (6), 420-422.
Summarizes some key research findings about motivation among junior high students.

Spires, Hiller A. & Stone, P. Diane. (1989). The Directed Notetaking Activity: A self-questioning approach. *Journal of Reading.* 33, (1), 36-39.
Suggests that students may benefit less from note-taking than they should because they have not brought much of the process to a conscious level. Offers a step-by-step guide for helping students take better notes and make more use of them for learning.

ACTIVE LEARNING

RECIPROCAL TEACHING is a powerful strategy. Students in a small group use the skills of predicting, questioning, clarifying and summarizing to interact with challenging material. Through the use of these four skills, the students learn how to set purposes for reading, how to critically evaluate and monitor themselves, and how to find the main idea in the text. The teacher initially models the interactive dialogue, with the students following the teacher's example, and engaging in the same activities.

This strategy is designed to help students focus on four specific comprehension strategies and actively use them in participating in and leading class discussions. It includes a teacher modeling component, and gradually, the teacher fades from control as students take over the discussion themselves.

Planning for a reciprocal teaching lesson has two phases. First, become familiar with the text selection by following this five-step procedure.

1. Identify which text segments will be used to demonstrate the four comprehension strategies.
2. Identify salient questions in the selection and generate additional questions about the material.
3. Generate possible predictions about each text segment.
4. Underline summarizing sentences and generate possible summaries for each text segment.
5. Circle difficult vocabulary or concepts.

Second, make two diagnostic decisions about the students who will participate.

1. Decide what strategies the students already use when reading and what is needed to help them learn from the text.
2. Evaluate the students' abilities to generate text questions, summarize, predict, and clarify, and decide what kind of support they will need to participate in and eventually lead each of these activities.

Instructional Procedure for Reciprocal Teaching Strategy

1. When reciprocal teaching is first introduced, the teacher and the students should discuss why the text may be difficult to understand, why strategies are important to help with the understanding and studying of the text and how reciprocal teaching will help the students monitor themselves as they read. Next, the students should be given an overall description of reciprocal teaching, and an explanation of the four strategies to be used. The explanations should include these four major comprehension strategies:

Summarizing - this gives the student the opportunity to identify and integrate the most important information in the text. The students begin by summarizing sentences, and with time and practice, progress to summarizing paragraphs and passages.

Question Generating - the students are deciding which information is important enough to provide the substance for a question. They can teach themselves to ask questions in which they must infer and apply new information from the text.

Clarifying - this skill is particularly helpful to those students who have trouble with comprehension. They come to realize that various factors, such as new vocabulary, unclear referent words, or difficult concepts, may make a text very hard to understand. Once they are taught to be alert to these factors, they can take the necessary steps to restore meaning.

Predicting - by using prediction, the students must activate their background knowledge, and have a purpose set for reading. They are then called upon to set a hypothesis about what the author will discuss next in the text. Reading to prove or disprove their hypothesis becomes a new purpose for reading. The students also learn that text structures provide clues as to what might happen next, through the use of headings, subheadings, and questions imbedded in the text.

2. The students should be given one day of practice for each of the four skills. For example, the students may practice summarization by summarizing their favorite movies or television shows. They then use the text to identify the main ideas in sentences, paragraphs, and eventually passages. The same type of instruction should be repeated for all of the skills.
3. After the students have been introduced to each of the skills, the teacher begins to introduce the students to the actual dialogue. On the first day of instruction, the teacher models reciprocal teaching. It is important that he or she calls on every student to participate at some level.
4. As the students become more familiar with the procedure, the teacher turns over the responsibility for the dialogue to them. He or she then becomes a coach, and provides the students with evaluative information, prompting them to more and higher levels of participation.

Palincsar, A.S., Ransom, K., & Derber, S. (1989). Collaborative research and development of reciprocal teaching. *Educational Leadership*, 46, (4), 37-40.

SONG-WRITING

Write a song to be sung to the tune, "Are You Sleeping," by completing the following form:

Who? (4 syllables) Repeat (same 4 syllables)	
Where was the character or idea at the beginning? (3 syllables) Think of 4 -ing words that describe this thing (12 syllables)	Where at the end? (3 syllables)
Summarize the main idea (3 syllables)	Repeat summary or add more summation (3 syllables)

Here's an example for the story of the *Three Little Pigs*:

> Big, mean wolfie: Big, mean wolfie
> At the door: In the pot
> Huffing, puffing, falling, stewing
> In the pot—
> Tough you're not!

Polette, Nancy. (1991). Whole Language in Action: Presented at the regular meeting of the Central Utah Reading Council, Orem, UT. Nancy can be contacted through the company Book Lures at: P.O. Box 9450, O'Fallon, MO 63366, telephone (800) 444-9450.

Study Guide: Chapter 8

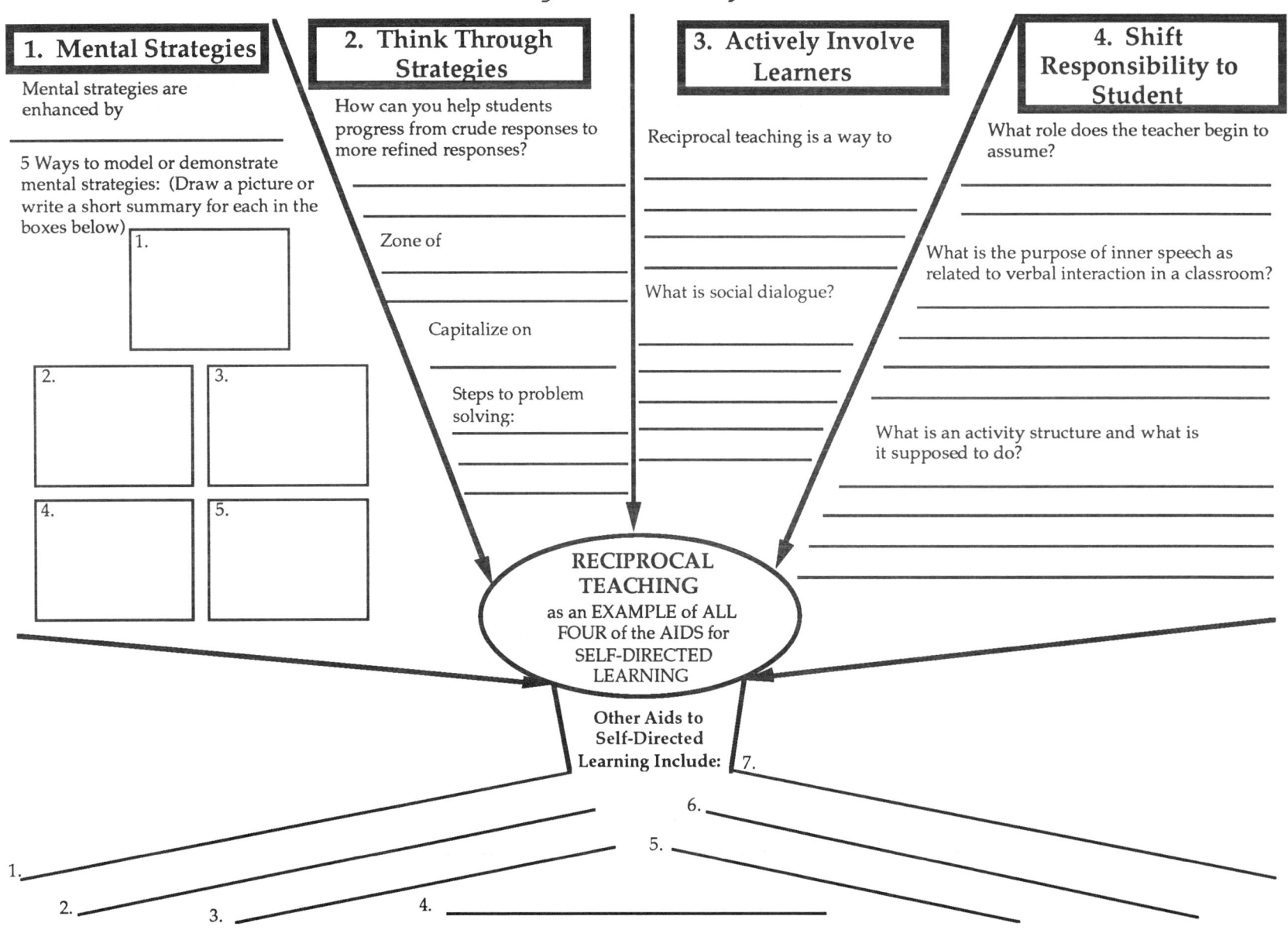

1. Mental Strategies

Mental strategies are enhanced by
_____

5 Ways to model or demonstrate mental strategies: (Draw a picture or write a short summary for each in the boxes below)

1.
2.
3.
4.
5.

2. Think Through Strategies

How can you help students progress from crude responses to more refined responses?
_____
_____

Zone of
_____
_____

Capitalize on
_____
_____

Steps to problem solving:
_____
_____

3. Actively Involve Learners

Reciprocal teaching is a way to
_____
_____
_____
_____

What is social dialogue?
_____
_____
_____
_____
_____

4. Shift Responsibility to Student

What role does the teacher begin to assume?
_____
_____
_____

What is the purpose of inner speech as related to verbal interaction in a classroom?
_____
_____
_____
_____

What is an activity structure and what is it supposed to do?
_____
_____
_____
_____

RECIPROCAL TEACHING as an EXAMPLE of ALL FOUR of the AIDS for SELF-DIRECTED LEARNING

Other Aids to Self-Directed Learning Include:

1. _____
2. _____
3. _____
4. _____
5. _____
6. _____
7. _____

BRIDGES

KNOWLEDGE — **ACTIVITY**

Chapter 10
Cooperative Learning and the Collaborative Process

Chapter 10	A. Personal, Dialogue, or Buddy Journals	B. Self-Directed Study Activities	C. Cooperative & Collaborative Ideas	D. Whole Class ☺☺☺☺☺☺
Introducing the Content	1. **REFLECT** on your experiences in working on projects in pairs or in groups. What was good? What was bad? What might you change? Why?	1. Think about yourself and **COMPLETE THE FOLLOWING STATEMENT**: "When it comes to working in groups, I prefer ___ because ___." **ELABORATE** on your ideas. How might your personal preferences relate to your teaching style and choices?	1. Working in pairs, **ADDRESS** the following questions: What does it mean to collaborate? To cooperate? **COMPLETE THE MOVEMENT ACTIVITY** (p. 71) to illustrate the two concepts. What implications do you see for teaching regarding the two ideas?	1. **MAKE TWO COLUMNS** on a chalkboard or overhead transparency. Head one column with the word "collaborative" and the other column with the word "cooperative". **BRAINSTORM** meanings for the two terms and **COMPARE** and **CONTRAST** them.

Chapter 10 Continued	A. Personal, Dialogue, or Buddy Journals	B. Self-Directed Study Activities	C. Cooperative & Collaborative Ideas	D. Whole Class
Assimilating /Reviewing the Content	2. How does the concept of structure relate to learners? Do learners "need" a structure? Structure in what? How much? 3. How do you feel about the statement "2 heads are better than one"? Is it true in learning? Are 2 or more heads ever less helpful? When?	2. **SKIM** work by Slavin (pp. 70 & 72) and **CHOOSE** a cooperative learning technique you like. **CRITIQUE** it, identifying its strengths, weaknesses, and best applications. **PRESENT** and "sell" this strategy to your peers, or **TEST IT OUT** in a teaching situation (if you are tutoring, etc.). What did you discover? 3. What would you **GUESS** are some of the most common errors teachers make in trying to implement cooperative learning strategies? How might a teacher avoid some of these errors?	2. **USE A JIGSAW FORMAT** (p. 72) to learn about the cooperative strategies summarized in this guide (or others which your instructor suggests).	2. If you have used collaborative or cooperative groups in the class, spend a few minutes **DISCUSSING** how these groups have worked and what strengths and weaknesses students have seen in their use. If you have not used these groups, ask students to **SHARE EXPERIENCES** from classes or courses where they have done so. **FOCUS** especially on what works well within such groups and what purposes are best achieved through collaborative and cooperative grouping.

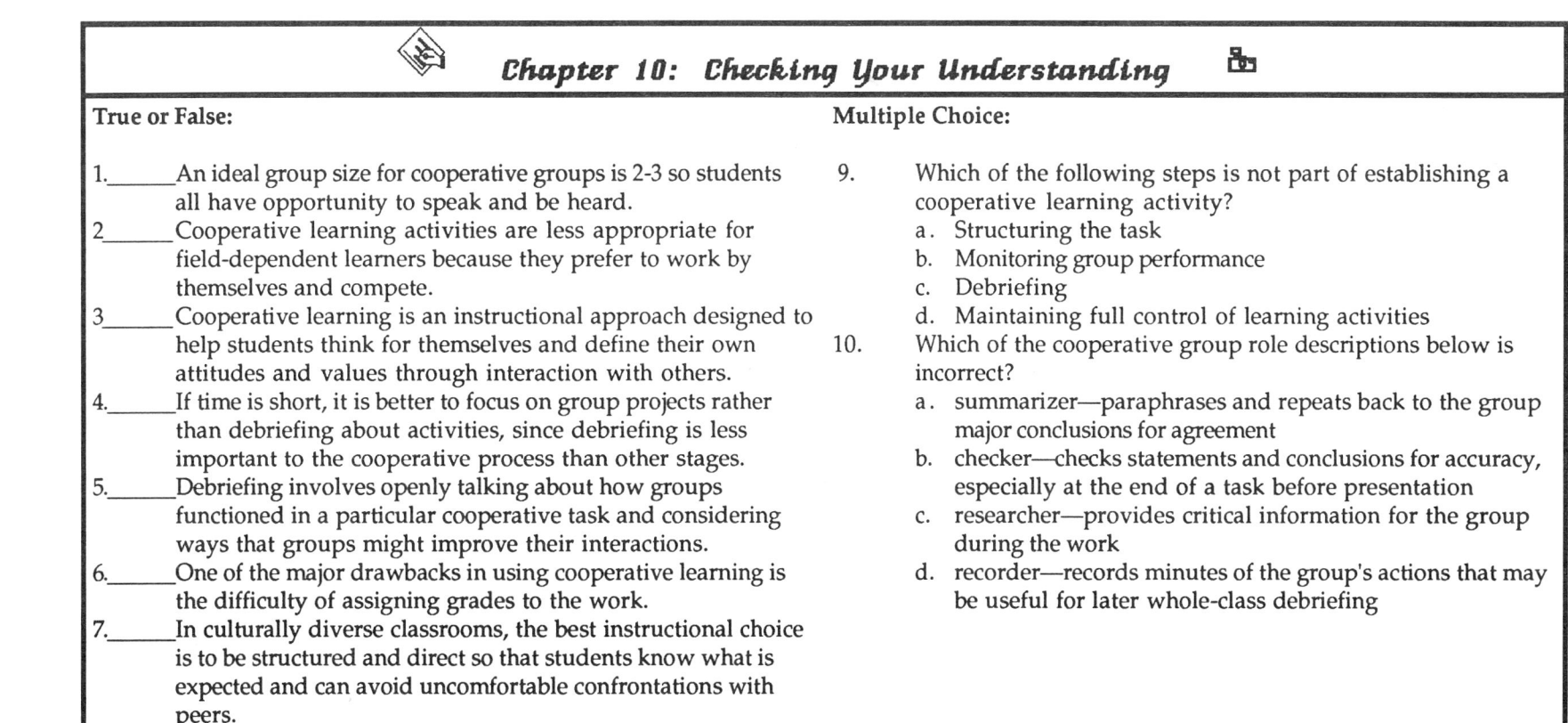

Chapter 10: Checking Your Understanding

True or False:

1. _____ An ideal group size for cooperative groups is 2-3 so students all have opportunity to speak and be heard.
2. _____ Cooperative learning activities are less appropriate for field-dependent learners because they prefer to work by themselves and compete.
3. _____ Cooperative learning is an instructional approach designed to help students think for themselves and define their own attitudes and values through interaction with others.
4. _____ If time is short, it is better to focus on group projects rather than debriefing about activities, since debriefing is less important to the cooperative process than other stages.
5. _____ Debriefing involves openly talking about how groups functioned in a particular cooperative task and considering ways that groups might improve their interactions.
6. _____ One of the major drawbacks in using cooperative learning is the difficulty of assigning grades to the work.
7. _____ In culturally diverse classrooms, the best instructional choice is to be structured and direct so that students know what is expected and can avoid uncomfortable confrontations with peers.
8. _____ Cooperative learning activities completed in teams encourage collaborative skills, self-esteem and achievement of individual learners.

Multiple Choice:

9. Which of the following steps is not part of establishing a cooperative learning activity?
   a. Structuring the task
   b. Monitoring group performance
   c. Debriefing
   d. Maintaining full control of learning activities

10. Which of the cooperative group role descriptions below is incorrect?
   a. summarizer—paraphrases and repeats back to the group major conclusions for agreement
   b. checker—checks statements and conclusions for accuracy, especially at the end of a task before presentation
   c. researcher—provides critical information for the group during the work
   d. recorder—records minutes of the group's actions that may be useful for later whole-class debriefing

1. F	2. F	3. T	4. F	5. T
6. F	7. F	8. T	9. d	10. d

Chapter 10: Performance Assessment Ideas

Individual	Small Group	Whole Class
1. WRITE about several ways you could assign roles within cooperative groups of students. Include advantages and disadvantages of each choice. 2. OBSERVE a lesson where cooperative or collaborative approaches are being used. INTERVIEW a student (with the teacher's and student's permission) for his or her perspective. WRITE a short summary of your experience.	1. BRAINSTORM 2-3 problems that might occur in cooperative or collaborative settings. WRITE a short scenario of each and include how you might solve each difficulty. 2. INTERVIEW a teacher who uses cooperative or collaborative grouping strategies regarding major advantages and disadvantages of these approaches. WRITE a brief summary of your experience.	1. DISCUSS as a class what strengths and weaknesses your group exhibits with respect to cooperation and collaboration. CHOOSE an area in which to improve and BRAINSTORM possible alternatives. RESOLVE as a class to implement an alternative and EVALUATE your progress in a week or two.

REFERENCES

Artzt, Alice F. (1994). Integrating writing and cooperative learning in the mathematics class. *The Mathematics Teacher.* 87, (2), 80-85.
The author describes activities used in teacher preparation classes which can be applied to teaching writing, mathematics, and cooperative learning in other grades.

Barnitz, John G. (1994). Discourse diversity: Principles for authentic talk and literacy instruction. *Journal of Reading.* 37, (7), 586-591.
Reviews selected studies on cultural variation of discourse and recommends 6 principles for teachers to help them use authentic talk in the classroom.

Brent, Rebecca & Anderson, Patricia. (1993). Developing children's classroom listening strategies. *The Reading Teacher.* 47, (2), 122-126.
Notes that students need to become good listeners to facilitate learning and communication. Suggests that teachers should model good listening, teach lessons in listening, and provide meaningful reasons for students to listen.

Kagan, Spencer. (1995). Group grades miss the mark. *Educational Leadership.* 52, (8), 68-71.
Explains that teachers should never give group grades for cooperative learning activities. Offers grading ideas and alternatives.

Kletzien, Sharon Benge & Baloche, Lynda. (1994). The shifting muffled sound of the pick: Facilitating student-to-student discussion. *Journal of Reading.* 37, (7), 540-545.
Offers ideas on structuring discussion activities within cooperative learning settings as well as in one-on-one interactions.

Mickel, Vesta L. (1993). Using cooperative learning in teaching content reading. *Journal of Reading.* 36, (8), 659-660.
Describes a specific strategy for having cooperative groups read new content area material.

O'Neal, Judy. (1990, March). Time for a change? *Teaching, K-8.* 56-57.
  A second grade teacher shares her experiences in transforming her classroom to facilitate cooperative learning.
Sinatra, Richard. (1991). Integrating whole language with the learning of text structure. *Journal of Reading.* 34, (6), 424-433.
  Suggests several ways middle school teachers can blend instruction in text structure with more holistic teaching approaches that foster communication, conceptualization, and collaboration.
Smith, Lana J. & Smith, Dennie L. (1994). The discussion process: A simulation. *Journal of Reading.* 37, (7), 582-585.
  Describes how to plan and implement a discussion simulation as a way to instruct students to achieve better discussions.
Vermette, Paul. (1994, September). The right start for cooperative learning. *Education Digest.* 35-38.
  Describes four traps to avoid in first using cooperative learning.
Wiencek, Joyce & O'Flahavan, John F. (1994). From teacher-led to peer discussions about literature: Suggestions for making the shift. *Language Arts.* 71, (7), 488-498.
  Addresses several questions teachers raise as they shift from teacher-led to student-led discussions.

ACTIVE LEARNING

MOVEMENT ACTIVITY
Students work in pairs. One is the sculptor, the other is to be "sculpted". The sculptor fashions the material into a statue depicting an emotion or event. At a signal from the instructor, sculptors stop and the sculptures "freeze". Sculptors move about the room and inspect the sculptures, guessing at the possible messages. Pairs can then trade roles. A second variation occurs when students work in groups of three. Now two sculptors create one sculpture, collaborating on the ideas. Students can then compare the differences in working alone as a sculptor and sculpting with a partner. (Teachers may play soft background music during "sculpting" to enhance the artistic mood of the experience.)

COOPERATIVE LEARNING

A. Jigsaw
Roles: Recorder, timer, spokesman, encourager, monitor (of interaction), reader
1. Number each team from 1-4.
2. Have all the 1's meet in a given area to read and discuss specific information.
3. Do the same with 2-4.
4. After a given amount of time, have numbered members return to their "home" teams to share the knowledge gained in each area.

B. Numbered Heads Together
1. Have students number off within groups, so that each student is a 1, 2, 3, or 4.
2. Ask a high-consensus questions, such as "When did Columbus sail?"
3. Tell the students to put their heads together to make sure everyone on the team knows the answer.
4. Call a number (1, 2, 3, or 4) and have all the students with that number share their answers (through writing on the chalkboard, writing on a paper and holding it up, etc.).
5. Continue with increasingly difficult questions. Keep "score" if so desired.

C. Roundtable
1. Ask a question with many possible answers.
2. Have students in groups make a list of all of their answers, with each person writing an answer on the paper and passing it to the next person.
3. The paper goes around the table until time is called, and then answers are shared and discussed.

An interesting variation of **Roundtable** is to send around four papers at a time so each person is always writing—or students can pass papers back and forth in pairs and when time is called, share their paper with the other pair in their group.

D. Roundrobin (Oral counterpart of Roundtable)
1. Ask a question with many possible answers.
2. Have each student take a turn (round robin reading style) providing an answer to the question.
3. When time is called, someone in the group summarizes ideas from the group.

E. Team Word-Webbing
1. Give each student a different color pen or marker and give the team one large poster paper, butcher paper, etc.
2. Have students write the main concept of your lesson in the center of the paper.
3. Have students think of words to add in roundtable style to the web.
4. Place webs at the front of the room and discuss interesting insights.

This can be completed before a lesson begins, and again at its conclusion to enhance connections and ideas. It can be part of a discussion starter, or simply the concluding activity to "bring together" ideas.

F. Student Teams Achievement Divisions (STAD)
Teams are formed to study for a test which students take when they feel each team member is ready. If each child attains his/her predetermined goal, the entire group is rewarded.

Kagan, Spencer. (1990). *Cooperative learning resources for teachers*. San Juan Capistrano, CA: Printing and Reprographics—University of California, Riverside.

Templeton, S. (1991). *Teaching the integrated language arts*. Boston: Houghton Mifflin, 107-109.

BRIDGES

Chapter 11
Group Process and Anticipatory Management

KNOWLEDGE — **ACTIVITY**

Chapter 11	A. Personal, Dialogue, or Buddy Journals	B. Self-Directed Study Activities	C. Cooperative & Collaborative Ideas	D. Whole Class
Introducing the Content	1. **THINK BACK** to teachers you consider competent or less competent. What were the differences? What cued you as to their abilities? 2. Do you ever act differently in one class than another? Why? Would you be embarrassed if your favorite teacher watched how you acted in your least favorite class? Why?	1. **MAP** your ideal classroom and **SUMMARIZE** your reasons for the arrangement of items. 2. **READ** the **CAR STORY** in the **ACTIVE LEARNING** section (p. 78). What insights do you gain from considering this story in relation to classroom management? In relation to coming to know and understand your students?	1. Form groups or pairs according to the grade level and setting in which you hope to teach and **BRAINSTORM** a set of rules for that grade. **SHARE** memories of experiences/rules you found personally effective before creating the list. 2. **BRAINSTORM** some ideas for smooth transitions between activities. 3. **BRAINSTORM** some good openings and closings for a particular lesson. Remember to consider lively poetry, etc. as good attention-getters (as noted in Chapter 5).	1. Have a clear opening and closing today and **POINT THEM OUT**. 2. Have students **SHARE** their "first day" of teaching fears. **SHARE** the **PORCUPINE STORY** (p. 78) and provide some concrete suggestions for the first day of class.

Chapter 11 Continued	A. Personal, Dialogue, or Buddy Journals	B. Self-Directed Study Activities	C. Cooperative & Collaborative Ideas	D. Whole Class
Assimilating /Reviewing the Content	3. **COMPARE AND CONTRAST** the words "classroom control" and "classroom management." What does each encompass with respect to an educational philosophy? What does each instill or preclude?	3. **REVIEW** the five types of social power. Where do you think you have strengths? **READ** in an area you'd like to strengthen and **SET A CONCRETE GOAL** for a way to grow there. 4. How do you plan to manage your classroom? What kind of classroom climate do you hope to create? Why? What are some steps you'll take to do this? Should you allow other climates? Why or why not?	4. **DISCUSS** with a partner the following question: Have you been part of a group that successfully achieved all four stages of development? **REFLECT** on how and why that happened and the implications from that experience for you as a teacher.* 5. **WRITE** a letter for parents that reflects your classroom management plan and intended class rules. **READ** it to a partner/group and make revisions.	3. **REFLECT** with students on effective and ineffective management strategies they have experienced over the years. **LINK** the discussion back to Chapter 1 engagement ideas: Discipline problems may occur because students are not engaged.

*Note: Because students learned about 6 different cooperative grouping strategies in Unit 10 (if you completed that activity), vary the grouping strategies here. Debrief not only on the activity content, but on how the group felt about the strategy.

Chapter 11: Checking Your Understanding

True or False:

1. _____ Teachers can do very little to influence classroom norms.
2. _____ The physical arrangement of a classroom contributes little to the overall social climate.
3. _____ In order to maintain professionalism, students should know as little as possible about the personal lives, interests, and ideas of their teachers.
4. _____ Referent power is the kind of influence a teacher gains with students when they feel their teacher is trustworthy, fair, and concerned about them as individuals.
5. _____ To enhance classroom management, it is important to wait for stragglers before beginning a new activity.
6. _____ If group members rebel against group norms, it is a sure sign that the norms were improperly established.
7. _____ One of the best ways to communicate "withitness" is through use of eye contact.
8. _____ Reward power is so strong that it eradicates the value of any other kind of teacher power in the classroom.
9. _____ It is helpful to display a listing of prior assignments somewhere in the classroom for students who miss class or need to make up work for some reason.
10. _____ Coercive power is the most effective type of social power teachers can use to establish a healthy and productive classroom environment.
11. _____ Competitive activities have little value in establishing or maintaining an effective classroom climate and should thus be avoided.
12. _____ Even if a lesson has gone well, closure is still important to help students remember what was learned and place it in perspective.

Multiple Choice:

13. Successful groups tend to pass through which of the following series of stages?
    a. Forming (acceptance); Storming (resolving concerns about shared influence); Norming (resolving concerns about work); Performing (resolving concerns about freedom, control, self-regulation)
    b. Forming (meeting one another); Storming (engaging in natural conflict); Norming (comparing the class against others); Performing (demonstrating achievement)
14. Which of the following are the most common reasons teachers experience difficulty in making transitions from one activity to another? (Mark all that apply)
    a. Learners are overly anxious to perform the next activity
    b. Learners are still working on the previous activity and are not ready to move to the next activity
    c. Learners have not been taught what to do during the transition
    d. Each transition is unique to its setting so learners must approach every one as a new experience

1. F	2. F	3. F	4. T	5. F	6. F	7. T
8. F	9. T	10. F	11. F	12. T	13. a	14. b, c

Chapter 11: Performance Assessment Ideas

Individual	*Small Group*	*Whole Class*
1. **RESPOND** to the **ASSESSMENT ACTIVITY** below (p. 78). 2. Use the **COOPERATIVE/COLLABORATIVE LEARNING PLANNING SHEET** (p. 79) to think through a cooperative/collaborative activity you'd like to teach. Complete the activity and reflect on its success as well as the helpfulness of the planning sheet. 3. According to the article below,[1] prospective teachers should try science strategies to build teaching confidence. How might (or does) this occur in your teacher preparation program? **SUMMARIZE** your ideas and **SUGGEST** possible changes to improve the experience.	1. **READ** the **GENERAL GUIDELINES FOR BEGINNING TEACHERS** (p. 80) and **RESPOND** to them. Are there any guidelines you would alter? Any you would add? Why or why not? **SUPPORT** for your ideas from your class text and other significant sources. 2. Moeller[2] suggests that academic success builds self-esteem rather than self-esteem building academic success. In some ways, this resembles the question of whether the chicken or the egg came first. **WHAT** do you think? Which comes first—academic success or self-esteem? **WHY** do you think so? How can you **DEFEND** your views? How might these views **TRANSLATE** into teaching practices?	1. **BRAINSTORM** how your group functions according to the stage descriptions in the text. In what areas is the group strong? In what areas might it improve?

CHILDREN'S LITERATURE CONNECTION

Krauss, Ruth. (1945). *The carrot seed.* **New York: Scholastic. (ISBN 0-590-00386-0)**
In this tried and true favorite, a little boy maintains his faith and patient care of a carrot seed until it produces an incredible harvest. In the same way, classroom management takes consistent effort and attention, and often grows from small seeds of routine and positive interaction. Further, the fact that the little boy persevered in his efforts to grow a carrot in spite of discouraging feedback may have stemmed partly from the fact of ownership: the carrot belonged to HIM. In like manner, classroom policies in which students have a voice and a stake are more likely to succeed.

REFERENCES

Adkins, Amee & Rogers, Dwight. (1994). "We don't have any rules. We have guidelines." *Teaching Education.* 6, (10), 145-148.
Two experienced third grade teachers reflect on how they manage their classrooms.

Chambers, Kevin. (1994). What makes a student improve? *Teaching Education.* 6, (1), 9-19.
An experienced, 7th grade world history teacher reflects on and researches about students motivation. Discovers that teacher influence is a big factor, especially when the teacher in interested in how students learn.

Elberfeld, Roy L. (1994, October). Bits of wisdom you just can't teach without. *Teaching K-8.* 66-67.
Lighthearted look at some things to remember at the year's beginning combined with some helpful ideas.

[1] **Enochs, Larry G.; Scharmann, Lawrence G.; & Riggs, Inis M.** (1995). The relationship of pupil control to preservice elementary science teacher self-efficacy and outcome expectancy. *Science Education.* 79, (1), 63-75.
Preservice teachers who expected to succeed at teaching science did—authors conclude that prospective teachers should be actively involved in teaching experience to build their confidence. Students should try strategies during early field experiences.

Fuhler, Carol J. (1994). Response journals: Just one more time with feeling. *Journal of Reading.* 37, (5), 400-405.
Discusses how she extended journals from her eighth grade classroom to involve the parents with positive results.

Greenwood, Scott C. (1995). Learning contracts and transaction: A natural marriage in the middle. *Language Arts.* 72, (2), 88-96.
Suggests that using learning contracts with middle school students can help build community as it builds language arts skill.

Howe, Ann C. (1994, Spring). How do you manage? *Science Activities.* 31, (1), 11-13.
Suggests that teachers need to think through managing hands-on science activities well before classtime to ensure success.

Johnson, David W. & Johnson, Roger T. (1993, December). Put gang dynamics on YOUR side! *Education Digest.* 35-38.
Explains how cooperative learning can meet students' needs in ways similar to those of gangs,—but with positive outcomes.

Klem, John. (No date.) *Motivating the unmotivated.* Phi Delta Kappa Educational Foundation Workshop Manual. Bloomington, Indiana: Phi Delta Kappa.
In this compilation of handouts from motivation seminar (presented across the nation), Klem hits on several points relating to student motivation which directly affect management issues.

Letts, Nancy. (1994, August/September). Building classroom unity. *Teaching K-8.* 106-107.
Short piece with numerous examples of ways to involve students in building a sense of community and establishing group norms.

[2] **Moeller, Thomas G.** (1994). What research says about self-esteem and academic performance. *Education Digest.* 34-37.
Notes that it may be better to help students build self-esteem by succeeding academically, rather than to attempt to build self-esteem to engender academic success.

Sharon L.; Garcia, Jesus; & Margalef-Boada, Sonia. (1994). Multicultural tradebooks in the social studies classroom. *The Social Studies.*
Students can come to know one another and avoid stereotyping through familiarity with a number of the books suggested in this article.

Weaver, Richard L, II; Wenzlaff, Sue; & Catrell, Howard W. (1993, October). How do students see master teachers? *Education Digest.* 12-15.
Traits students identified in several master teachers included having high standards/expectations and strong commitment to one's topic and job.

ACTIVE LEARNING

CAR STORY
   The story is told of a man who, while driving his Mercedes at high speeds up a mountain road, was forced to slow down as a woman approached him from a blind curve—driving on HIS SIDE of the road.
   Peeved, he swerved to miss her.
   As the two cars passed, she called out, "Cow!"
   Fuming, he took in her ample form, and responded, "Pig!"
   Just then, he rounded the curve, only to crash headlong into a huge cow.

PORCUPINE STORY
Share this story with students to begin a discussion about how each person's behavior in a classroom affects the other students. Young students can later recall the discussion (along with class behavior rules) by simple reminders such as: "Remember the porcupines," or "Be sure you're not being a porcupine."

Philosopher Arthur Schopenhauer tells the following story which illustrates nicely the challenge in becoming close enough with others to survive and get along, and yet maintaining the "distance" of manners and propriety which provides a sense of safety:
   "On a cold winter's day, a group of porcupines huddled together to stay warm and keep from freezing. But soon they felt one another's quills and moved apart. When the need for warmth brought them closer together again, their quills again forced them apart. They were driven back and forth at the mercy of their discomforts until they found the distance from one another that provided both a maximum of warmth and a minimum of pain.
   In human beings, the emptiness and monotony of the isolated self produces a need for society. This brings people together, but their many offensive qualities and intolerable faults drive them apart again. The optimum distance that they finally find and that permits them to coexist is embodied in politeness and good manners. Because of this distance between us, we can only partially satisfy our need for warmth, but at the same time, we are spared the stab of one another's quills."

Schopenhauer, Arthur. (1989). "Points to Ponder." *Reader's Digest*. 182.

Note: After sharing this story, you may want to return to the Gagne or Hunter lesson plan and add a reminder about management challenges. Plan how you will assign and monitor work, interact with students, reach special needs students, etc.

ASSESSMENT ACTIVITY
John Klem believes that a stressed teacher can't get past himself or herself to motivate the students. He claims that teachers must deal with their personal stress before they can focus on the classroom. Given what you have read, experienced, and discussed (especially pertaining to this course) respond to Klem's comments. If you agree with Klem, summarize your thinking and support it. Then take the opposite view and articulate a "devil's advocate" position. Conclude your response by attempting to refute the opposing view, supported with appropriate sources. If you disagree with Klem, reverse the steps listed above—first challenge his view, then seek to find strengths in his view, and finally, seek to refute those strengths, citing appropriate sources.

Cooperative/Collaborative Learning Planning Sheet

Think About:	Description	My Plan
Group Size	4-member groups are ideal	
Group Assignment	What are you going to have them investigate or do?	
Room Arrangement	Can people interact easily?	
Materials: Plan & Distribute	What will they need to work with and how will you distribute it?	
Assigning Roles	Who will do what within each group: Recorder, Timer, Encourager, Reader, Reporter, Monitor, etc.	
Explaining the Task	Write a quick summary and make it as clear as possible.	
Structuring Accountability	How will they (and you) know the task is complete and at what quality level?	
Structuring Group Cooperation	Why should they work together? Is a group format really best for this activity? Are they comfortable with one another?	
Criteria for Success	Exactly what is to be accomplished?	
Specifying Desired Behaviors	Tell them how you'd like them to interact with one another, not only socially, but academically.	
Monitoring	Plan to move around, listen, and help.	
Providing Assistance	Think of ways you could help groups who get "stuck".	
Closure of Lesson	Link group reports/activities clearly into the lesson and/or lesson summary.	
Assessing Student Learning	What did students gain from the lesson? e.g., "I learned . . ." slips or comments.	
Assessing Group Functioning	Have students share how well their groups worked and what they're learning about working together.	

General Guidelines for Beginning Teachers

Some general rules for starting off the year right:	Things to do before the first day of school:	That first morning:	During the first few weeks:
Be firm but fair from the start. Know your students. Plan your work carefully. Observe other teachers. Start slowly. Establish routines. Set standards. Be patient. Be calm. Do not do paperwork in class. Keep a sense of humor. Accept and try suggestions. Keep up professionally.	Check your administrative manual. Know your building. Get to know your supervisors. Make your room attractive. Get materials ready for the first day. Make a temporary room arrangement. Make a program for the first week, knowing you will probably alter it later.	Arrive early. Think over the three tasks you need to accomplish in the first few days: establish room control, set up good work habits, teach group cooperation. Greet students with a smile. Have your name on the chalkboard. Get students right into an activity. Make opening exercises brief. Check attendance. Develop room standards. Follow plans so students will feel they accomplished something the first day.	Maintain management. Study students' cumulative folders. Take advantage of every opportunity to meet parents. Begin a worthwhile class project. Record plenty of observations and grades. Spend sufficient time in lesson preparation: this will seem unusually long at first, but will grow shorter. Take advantage of available help (principal, specialists in the building, media center personnel, district personnel, etc.). Take advantage of professional meetings.

In addition: Think about transitions from one activity/lesson to another, the "short time periods at the beginning and end of the day, before and after recesses, and between lessons" during which "80 percent of all classroom management problems occur" (Templeton, 1991, pp. 90-91):

How are lunch money, teacher notes, homework, book orders, etc., to be handled? Can some of the burden be transferred FROM the teacher? Can students begin the day by reading silently or writing in dialogue/buddy journals while the teacher does required business? Are there routines for work collection and materials distribution? What about students who complete assignments? How will you close the day?

Starting the Year Right. (1978). *Instructor*. Dept. A34, Dansville, NY 14437.
Templeton, S. (1991). *Teaching the integrated language arts*. Boston: Houghton Mifflin, 90-91.

BRIDGES

Chapter 12
Classroom Order and Discipline

KNOWLEDGE — **ACTIVITY**

Chapter 12	A. Personal, Dialogue, or Buddy Journals	B. Self-Directed Study Activities	C. Cooperative & Collaborative Ideas	D. Whole Class
Introducing the Content	1. WRITE about some memories of punishment and/or reward in class and their effects. 2. What motivates you academically? Has that changed over the years? How?	1. What does the term "negative reinforcement" mean to you? SKIM the chapter to see how your definition COMPARES with that of the text. 2. READ or SKIM *Discipline With Dignity* or another management text. What do you think of the major points in the text? 3. WRITE an imaginary letter to your students' parents explaining your discipline plan (if you didn't do this for Chapter 11). If you are teaching now (i.e., student teaching, observing, etc.) address it to your assigned grade level.	1. BRAINSTORM classroom rules, interventions, and/or situations you recall as particularly effective or ineffective. CONSIDER why you think these occurred. 2. CREATE A SONG to SUMMARIZE either your "rules" or the woes of classroom discipline and management. You may want to try Polette's idea (p. 65) or *Animal Piggyback Songs*.[1]	1. BRAINSTORM meanings for the term "negative reinforcement". EXAMINE how this differentiation applies to teaching. 2. If you didn't use it for the introductory lesson, introduce this chapter by sharing the poem "Rules" by Karla Kuskin.[2] BRAINSTORM with the class several generic rules and consequences. CONSIDER natural versus contrived consequences.

81

Chapter 12 Continued	A. Personal, Dialogue, or Buddy Journals	B. Self-Directed Study Activities	C. Cooperative & Collaborative Ideas	D. Whole Class
Assimilating /Reviewing the Content	3. Did you ever break a rule and experience natural consequences as opposed to imposed consequences? How do these differ? Is one experience more effective? For what?	4. ADD management considerations to a previous lesson plan you have written or seen. SHARE your changes with your instructor or a small group. 5. CONSIDER the three management views discussed in Chapter 12. Have you experienced any or all of them? What implications might your experiences have for your future teaching decisions? 6. Think of a possible classroom rule. Frame it as a fun song or poem that could be used in class to remind students of the idea in a fun way. (See **RULE SONG**, p. 85, for an example.)	3. BRAINSTORM cultural experiences relating to management. 4 ROLE PLAY for the class an intervention from the 3 perspectives: behavior modification, humanist, classroom management. DISCUSS how these differed and what was most effective. 5. BRAINSTORM some management "blame" messages. Work in groups to CORRECT these messages to "sane" ones. SHARE.	3. Obtain 2 copies of the book *Discipline With Dignity* (or another favorite management book) and complete the **READ-A-BOOK-IN-AN-HOUR** activity (p. 85).

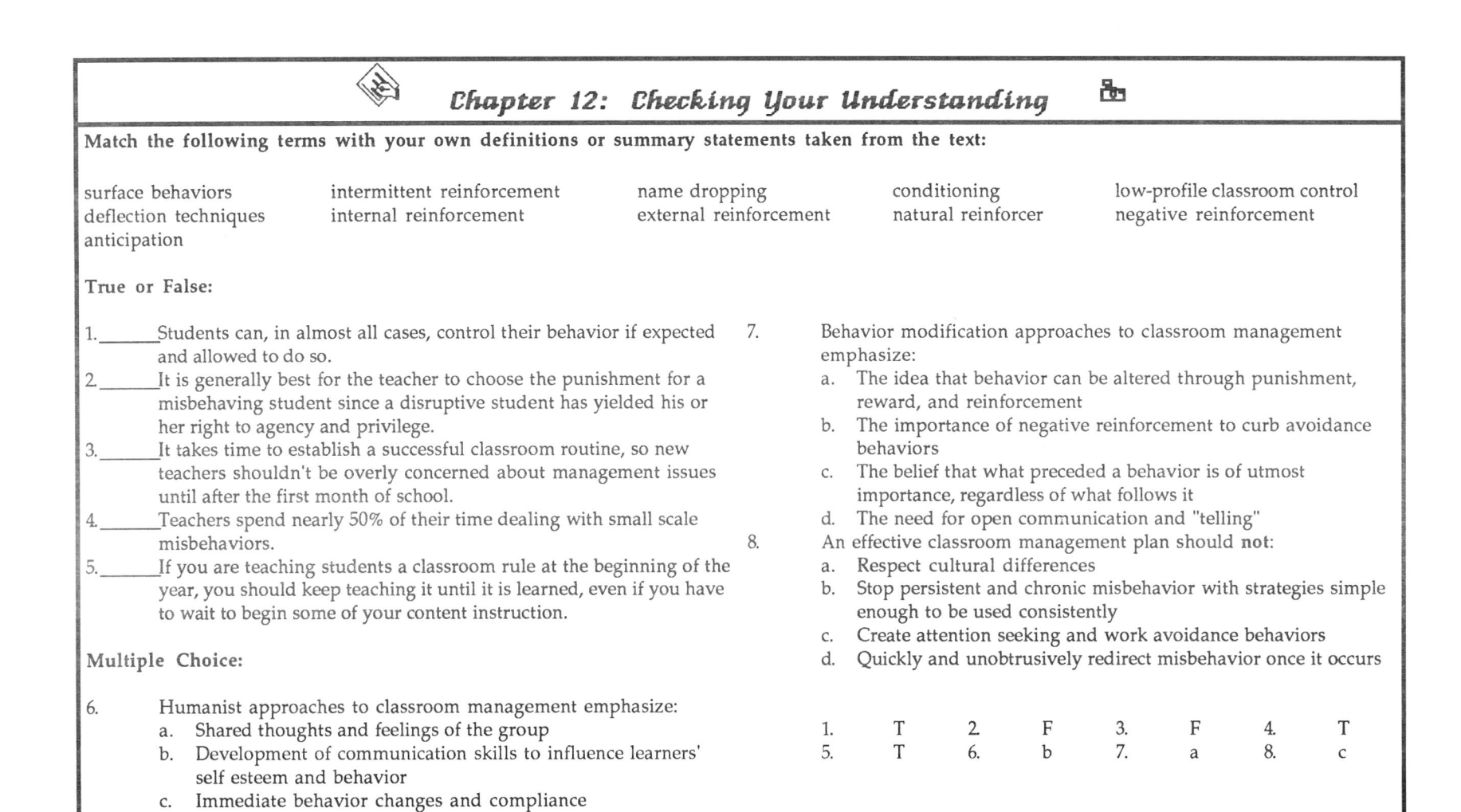

Chapter 12: Checking Your Understanding

Match the following terms with your own definitions or summary statements taken from the text:

surface behaviors	intermittent reinforcement	name dropping	conditioning	low-profile classroom control
deflection techniques	internal reinforcement	external reinforcement	natural reinforcer	negative reinforcement
anticipation				

True or False:

1. _____ Students can, in almost all cases, control their behavior if expected and allowed to do so.
2. _____ It is generally best for the teacher to choose the punishment for a misbehaving student since a disruptive student has yielded his or her right to agency and privilege.
3. _____ It takes time to establish a successful classroom routine, so new teachers shouldn't be overly concerned about management issues until after the first month of school.
4. _____ Teachers spend nearly 50% of their time dealing with small scale misbehaviors.
5. _____ If you are teaching students a classroom rule at the beginning of the year, you should keep teaching it until it is learned, even if you have to wait to begin some of your content instruction.

Multiple Choice:

6. Humanist approaches to classroom management emphasize:
   a. Shared thoughts and feelings of the group
   b. Development of communication skills to influence learners' self esteem and behavior
   c. Immediate behavior changes and compliance
   d. Recognition that group power is more important than individual will

7. Behavior modification approaches to classroom management emphasize:
   a. The idea that behavior can be altered through punishment, reward, and reinforcement
   b. The importance of negative reinforcement to curb avoidance behaviors
   c. The belief that what preceded a behavior is of utmost importance, regardless of what follows it
   d. The need for open communication and "telling"

8. An effective classroom management plan should **not**:
   a. Respect cultural differences
   b. Stop persistent and chronic misbehavior with strategies simple enough to be used consistently
   c. Create attention seeking and work avoidance behaviors
   d. Quickly and unobtrusively redirect misbehavior once it occurs

1. T   2. F   3. F   4. T
5. T   6. b   7. a   8. c

Chapter 12: Performance Assessment Ideas

Individual	Small Group	Whole Class
1. What are your greatest management concerns? How do you plan to **ADDRESS** them? **LIST** 3-5 concerns and 2-3 sources (for each concern) to which you might go to address these challenges if you need more help.	1. Work together in small groups to **CREATE** a poem, lyrics to a song, etc. to **SUMMARIZE** key concepts in the chapter. (See example in **ACTIVE LEARNING** section, p. 85.)	1. **BRAINSTORM** potential management problems for a particular grade and setting. **CHART** ways in which each management problem might be handled, **LISTING** the strengths and weaknesses of each choice.

REFERENCES

Curwin, Richard L., & Mendler, Allen N. (1988). *Discipline with dignity.* Association for Supervision and Curriculum Development.
Describes an approach to classroom management which respects each student as a responsible choice-maker.

Fisher, Bobbi. (1994, August/September). Getting democracy into first grade—or any grade. *Teaching K-8.* 87-89,
Well-known teacher describes her use of various student committees to manage her classroom.

Mercure, Christine M. (1994, December). Elementary schools' answers to corporal punishment. *Education Digest.* 25-28.
Shares management strategies from all over America.

Templeton, S. (1991). *Teaching the integrated language arts.* Boston: Houghton Mifflin, 101.
Includes some ideas for daily schedule for a self-contained elementary classroom. Ideas could be adapted for other elementary settings and may provide a frame from which to plan your own schedule.

Warren, Jean (compiler). (1990). *Animal piggyback songs.* Everett, Washington: Warren Publishing House, Inc. (ISBN 0-911019-29-4)
Includes a number of lyrics about animals written to be sung to familiar tunes such as "Row, Row, Row Your Boat," etc. A mailing address for this company is P. O. Box 2250, Everett, WA 98203.

ACTIVE LEARNING

RULE SONG
The following rule about not chewing gum in class could be sung to the tune of "Row, Row, Row Your Boat":

> Stow, stow, stow your gum,
> When you come to school.
> Chew it anywhere but here,
> That's a cardinal rule.

READ-A-BOOK-IN-AN-HOUR
Tear out the chapters of a paperback book and distribute them to individuals, pairs, or groups of students. Students read their sections silently or orally together. Students summarize their section orally together and rehearse what they will tell the large group (whole class) about their section. (Allow 15-20 minutes for reading and 3-5 minutes for students to summarize the section.) Students may make notes for final presentation. Allow students to present their sections numerically or obliterate section/chapter numbers and have students attempt to place their section/chapter in relation to other sections/chapters presented. If students "guess" where their section falls, have them 1) speculate about content covered in the previous chapter, and and 2) predict content in the next chapter when they meet in their groups. Begin the whole class sharing by asking, "Who thinks they have the first section/chapter? Why?" and continue on until the sections/chapters are in order and the books is summarized.

Bromley, K. D. (1992). *Language arts exploring connections*. Second Ed. Boston: Allyn & Bacon, 217.

ASSESSMENT ACTIVITY
For example, the following lyrics could be sung to the tune, "Jingle Bells" and summarize some of the chapter concepts:

First Verse:

Dashing through the halls,
Late for class again,
Drawing on the walls with a red felt pen.
Passing notes in class,
Sleeping in their chairs,
Failing to complete their work,
I'm tearing out my hairs!

Chorus:

My students have the best of me—
What am I to do?
I make the rules, they laugh at me;
I feel an utter fool!
Where's the magic remedy for my classroom woes?
It's anticipatory management,
And staying on my toes!

Second Verse:

Group dynamics, growth and change,
This I need to know:
And I need to realize how groups can work and grow.
Reinforcement and reward,
Carefully dispensed,
And whenever possible, natural consequence!

Repeat Chorus.

BRIDGES

Chapter 13: Teaching Special Learners in the Regular Classroom

KNOWLEDGE ——— **ACTIVITY**

Chapter 13	A. Personal, Dialogue, or Buddy Journals	B. Self-Directed Study Activities	C. Cooperative & Collaborative Ideas	D. Whole Class
Introducing the Content	1. Who are the special learners in a classroom? What is special about them? 2. How do you feel about "pull-out" and mainstream programs? What do you see as advantages or disadvantages? Do you have experience with any of these?	1. What are your views on pull-out and inclusive programs? Can you substantiate any claims you make within these views? **MAKE A CASE** for a particular practice and **SUPPORT** your views with professional sources. 2. **ATTEND** a school board meeting or **FOLLOW** the newspapers in you community during the next 2-3 weeks. Are any of the issues in this chapter being discussed in your community? What is being said/done? What do you think of what you're seeing/hearing?	1. **BRAINSTORM** types of disabilities and/or special needs you may encounter as a teacher and things to do/avoid in dealing with such needs in the classroom.	1. **ASK** students to **LOOK BACK** at the **INTEREST INVENTORY** (p. xi) and think of ways their interests may have been addressed in this course. **DISCUSS** ways to incorporate student interests in any course (i.e., referring to their hobbies, drawing examples from their lives, etc.). 2. **DISPLAY** an overhead transparency of a bell curve. **DISCUSS** where the "average" is on the curve, and what kinds of things occur in this distribution (height, weight, etc.). **RESPOND** to the idea of "average" intelligence and how that may or may not be an accurate view of intelligence.

86

Chapter 13 Continued	A. Personal, Dialogue, or Buddy Journals	B. Self-Directed Study Activities	C. Cooperative & Collaborative Ideas	D. Whole Class
Assimilating /Reviewing the Content	3. What is an "average" child? How many of these have you known or will you teach? Why do you think this? 4. What is a disability? How does it influence your teaching decisions?	3. READ any article referenced in this chapter and RESPOND to the author's position. 4 THINK ABOUT issues relating to the Family Privacy Act, diverse community backgrounds, and the talk that occurs in classrooms. If, in a sense, we are all "bilingual" by virtue of membership in more than one community (i.e., home, church, academic, peers, etc.), what does that bilingualism mean for teaching? How do we capitalize on/provide for the communicative diversity that can/will exist in our classrooms?	2. PRETEND you are a member of a faculty at a school where some students do not speak English (or the dominant language of that school). DEBATE the issue of which approach is best for dealing with your students. SEEK to settle on a CONSENSUS as a group. PRESENT your decision and SUPPORT to the class as you might present at a faculty or PTA meeting.	3. PREPARE for and HOLD a class mini-DEBATE on the issue of inclusion, tracking, or another "hot" topic in this chapter.

Chapter 13: Checking Your Understanding

Match the following terms with your own definitions or summary statements taken from the text:

limited English proficiency
mainstream
bilingual instruction

least restrictive environment
individual education plan

transition approach
maintenance approach

enrichment approach
restoration approach

True or False:

1. _____ One way ability grouping may be important and helpful to gifted learners is when gifted and talented students are grouped together to pursue accelerated programs for skipping grades and obtaining college credit.
2. _____ An at-risk learner is mentally retarded, emotionally disturbed, or requires continual disciplining.
3. _____ Bilingualism decisions are crucial because a child's later language competence can be severely impaired if s/he is taught more than one language at too early an age.
4. _____ Remedial teaching is designed to eliminate weaknesses and deficiencies learners have.
5. _____ A high IQ score is a sure sign of giftedness.
6. _____ Languages vary in their complexity and usefulness for learning and problem solving; thus, it is better for students to learn a "harder" language like English to promote cognitive development.
7. _____ Special learners are classified according to categories to help teachers remember the learners' characteristics.
8. _____ Compensatory teaching means to alter a presentation of content to circumvent or work around a student's fundamental weakness or deficiency.
9. _____ Teachers prefer teaching gifted learners because they are easier to teach than at-risk students.

Multiple Choice:

10. Teachers can meet many special needs of students through which of the following approaches? (Mark all that apply)
    a. encourage interaction between regular and special learners
    b. use a formal classroom arrangement to decrease distractions
    c. use computer software for remedial instruction
    d. encourage self-management skills in students
11. Which of the following is **not** an instructional strategy recommended for addressing the learning needs of at-risk students?
    a. provide study aids that highlight important content
    b. teach learning strategies which can be used across a variety of subjects, such as notetaking, self-monitoring, vocal rehearsal
    c. develop lessons around students' interests, needs, and experiences
    d. use oral expression instead of written expression in assignments
12. Which of the following strategies is **not** recommended for teaching gifted learners among regular students?
    a. plan occasional group activities
    b. plan activities which include freedom of choice and opportunity to pursue personal interests
    c. draw upon real-life problems for classroom work
    d. minimize the role of testing and questioning in favor of nonevaluative activities

1. T   2. F   3. F   4. T   5. F   6. F   7. F   8. T   9. F   10. a, c, d   11. d   12. d

Chapter 13: Performance Assessment Ideas		
Individual	*Small Group*	*Whole Class*
1. Reflect on a classroom experience involving a special needs learner. What needs did the student have? How were they met or unmet? What would you do differently as a result of your study in this course?	1. Are gifted students also "special needs" students? Should they receive special attention and consideration? **RESPOND** to the information on "gifted" learners (p. 91-92). **SUPPORT** your views with appropriate sources.	1. **INVITE** a guest to address the class who has worked with special needs students. **PREPARE** questions in advance for the speaker. After the presentation, **DISCUSS** the speaker's major points and **WRITE** a reflection on the experience.

CHILDREN'S LITERATURE CONNECTION

Geisel, Theodor S. (Dr. Seuss). (1979). *Oh say can you say?* New York: Random House, Inc. (ISBN 0-394-84255-3)
   This book of extended tongue twisters provides an entertaining look at the power and challenge of language—offering an interesting introduction to thinking about different discourse communities and language abilities among the special learners in our classrooms.

Gwynne, Fred. (1976). *A chocolate moose for dinner.* New York: Trumpet Club. (ISBN 0-440-84330-8)
   Highlights how confusing homonyms in our language can be. May help us be more forbearing with students who speak English as a second language.

Parish, Peggy. (1963). *Amelia Bedelia.* New York: Harper & Row. (ISBN 0-06-443036-7)
   Delightful look at the difficulties encountered by Amelia Bedelia, a maid who takes everything literally. Helpful in highlighting how confusing idioms and other figures of speech can be if one lacks background experience for translating them.

REFERENCES

Bergman, Janet L. (1992). SAIL—A way to success and independence for low-achieving readers. *The Reading Teacher.* 45, (8), 598-602.
   Describes the goals of the SAIL program (Students Achieving Independent Learning) and how students learn important strategies through participation in SAIL. Readers may be particularly interested in this article if SAIL is being used in nearby school districts.

Curwin, Richard. (1994, October). Teaching at-riskers how to cope. *Education Digest.* 11-15.
   Provides ten suggestions for helping at-risk students feel more comfortable in class.

Dana, Carol. (1989). Strategy families for disabled readers. *Journal of Reading.* 33, (1), 30-35.
   Summarizes a number of strategies for helping students improve their reading skills and comprehension before, during, and after reading. Includes suggestions on how to teach strategies to students.

Educational Leadership. (1995, December/January). 52, (4).
Complete issue is dedicated to the topic of inclusion.

Fiedler, Ellen D.; Lange, Richard E.; & Winebrenner, Susan. (1994, January). Ability grouping: Geared for the gifted. *Education Digest.* 52-55.
Makes distinctions between tracking and ability grouping and attempts to debunk six "myths" about ability grouping.

Fitzgerald, Jill. (1993). Literacy and students who are learning English as a second language. *The Reading Teacher.* 46, (8), 638-647.
Raises several common questions regarding ESL instruction and summarizes practice, research, and theory addressing these questions.

Friend, Marilyn & Cook, Lynne. (1993, November/December). Inclusion. *Instructor.* 53-56.
Discusses what is meant by the term inclusion and what makes inclusion succeed.

Gersten, Russell & Jimenez, Robert T. (1994). A delicate balance: Enhancing literature instruction for students of English as a second language. *The Reading Teacher.* 47, (6), 438-449.
A study of three different teachers and their ESL instruction suggests several useful instructional practices. One of the three teachers is a first-year teacher, and thus, may be particularly interesting to readers.

Long, Nicholas J. (1995, May). Inclusion: Formula for failure? *Education Digest.* 26-29.
Discusses some of the complexities of inclusion.

McKeon, M. (1994). Reversing the trend of failure for children with emotional and behavioral difficulties (EBD): The role of science. *School Science Review.* 76, (275), 109-112.
Notes that science can be a helpful intervention for providing many of the learning experiences recommended for children with behavioral and emotional challenges.

Mohr, Kathleen A. J. (1994, May). Making a PLACE for foreign students in class. *Education Digest.* 44-48.
Uses the acronym PLACE to discuss 5 suggested categories for teaching students who speak languages other than English.

Rekrut, Martha D. (1994). Peer and cross-age tutoring: The lessons of research. *Journal of Reading.* 37, (5), 356-362.
Notes that with a growing interest in cooperative and collaborate learning, teachers need to consider how each strategy best supports students in their learning. Although this article focuses on helping students read better, the questions about various instructional approaches are important for any discipline.

Reyes, Maria de la Luz & Molner, Linda A. (1991). Instructional strategies for second-language learners in the content areas. *Journal of Reading.* 35, (2), 96-103.
Reviews a number of strategies for helping language minority students deal with literacy tasks. Strategies are only recommended if they have been tested within a language minority setting.

Zucker, Carol. (1993). Using whole language with students who have language and learning disabilities. *The Reading Teacher.* 46, (8), 660-670.
Suggests that a whole language approach benefits students with special needs. Describes an actual program implementation and some of its results.

Gifted Students

Tompkins and Hoskisson (1991) suggest that teachers should work with mainstreamed gifted students primarily through independent study assignments. In designing independent study activities, they believe a teacher must consider the following variables:

Pacing	Instruction for gifted students should be rapidly paced to suit their learning style.
Level of abstraction	Gifted students can engage in hypothetical reasoning, discuss complex issues, make higher order inferences, and utilize systematic procedures in their quest for knowledge.
Type of subject matter	Interdisciplinary units are well suited to the complex minds and synthesizing abilities of the gifted.
Depth of study	For gifted students, depth is preferable to breadth.
Range of resources	Gifted students can be given access to a greater variety and more advanced level or resources than the norm. Human resources should also be used to a greater extent.
Dissemination	High quality student products should be shared with the community in some way.

What do you think?

Tompkins, G.E. & Hoskisson, K. (1991). *Language arts content and teaching strategies.* New York: Merrill, 588.

Gifted Students

In a compilation of research on teaching the English Language Arts, the editors note that many times verbally talented students actually become "at-risk" because when a student sees relationships unforeseen by the teacher, the teacher may respond as if the child is incorrect or inappropriately responding. These students also often miss answers on standardized tests because they can see so many possibilities for many of the answers. The research also suggests that teachers may encounter the following difficulties with students having certain characteristics:

Characteristic	Example Difficulty	Characteristic	Example Difficulty
Critical Thinking	Is reluctant to submit work that is not perfect; may not even begin a project because of feeling that it may not reach one's own excessively high standards; criticizes peers and teachers, causing negative reactions and feelings	High Verbal Ability	Dominates class and informal discussion; is sarcastic of others; argues for the sake of argument, detracting from the progress of the lesson; uses humor not always understood or accepted by others
Abstract Thinking	Neglects details once generalizations are mastered; jumps to conclusions about specifics; impatient with teacher's focus on specific steps or details in a procedure; becomes frustrated by others' inability to understand general concepts quickly; designs own procedures that may be in conflict with those taught by the teacher	Questioning	Continually raises questions that sometime interfere with the teacher's lesson; needs access to a variety of materials
		Persistence	Focuses on areas of personal interest, sometimes at the expense of work in other areas often required by the teacher; is viewed as stubborn

They suggest that in working with gifted students, teachers should:

1. Focus on and be organized to provide more elaborate, complex, and in-depth study of major ideas, problems, and themes that integrate knowledge with and across systems of thought.
2. Allow for the development and application of productive thinking skills to enable students to reconceptualize existing knowledge and generate new knowledge.
3. Enable them to explore constantly changing knowledge and information and develop the attitude that knowledge is worth pursuing in an open world.
4. Encourage exposure to selection, and use of appropriate and specialized resources.
5. Promote self-initiated and self-directed learning and growth.
6. Provide for the development of self-understandings and the understandings of one's relationship to persons, societal institutions, nature and culture.

What do you think?

Flood, J.; Jensen, J. M.; Lapp, D.; & Squire, J. R. (1991). *Handbook of research on teaching the English language arts.* New York: Macmillan, 375.

BRIDGES

Chapter 14
Assessing Learners: Objective and Essay Tests

KNOWLEDGE — **ACTIVITY**

Chapter 14	A. Personal, Dialogue, or Buddy Journals	B. Self-Directed Study Activities	C. Cooperative & Collaborative Ideas	D. Whole Class
Introducing the Content	1. REFLECT on memories of objective and standardized tests. Were you ever denied something or did you ever receive a grade that was not reflective of your ability/knowledge? 2. What does it mean to be test-wise? Can that be taught? Should it be taught? 3. COMPLETE the TRADITIONAL PRACTICE QUESTIONS as an ANTICIPATION GUIDE (p. 6) for this chapter.	1. LIST your test strategies for the following types of questions: T/F Multiple Choice Fill in Short answer/essay 2. Do you see any value in pre- and post-testing? What pros and cons do you see?	1. With a partner, BRAINSTORM 3-5 poorly written test questions. TRADE your questions with those of another pair. IMPROVE the other group's questions. Do a THINK, PAIR, SHARE (p. 6) to review the questions and changes. CHOOSE one or two good questions and WRITE the first and second versions on clear acetate to SHARE with the whole class. 2. BRAINSTORM with the group the meaning of "mastery." How do you know when someone has "mastered" something?	1. DISPLAY an overhead transparency of a camera. ASK students to imagine you sneaking into their apartments at an odd hour of the day or night and snapping a photo of them while they slept. IMAGINE blowing it up to poster size and using it to introduce them to someone new, to determine a job application, etc. ASK what kind of information this photo would include? What is accurate? Inaccurate? How would they alter the situation to give a more "complete picture" of themselves? LINK to the idea of assessment and "one-time" snapshots of a child's performance on a certain task in a certain setting at a certain point.

Chapter 14 Continued	A. Personal, Dialogue, or Buddy Journals	B. Self-Directed Study Activities	C. Cooperative & Collaborative Ideas	D. Whole Class
Assimilating /Reviewing the Content	4. How do you study for a test? What information do you tend to retain after the test is over? 5. What is the relationship between assessment and self-esteem? Should it be this way? How would you alter it?	3. DESIGN a test for something in class or something you are/or will be teaching. REFLECT on your design and make changes after reading this chapter.	3. DEVISE a way (in small groups) you'd like your instructor to "test" you on this chapter. PRESENT your idea to the class, along with a rationale supporting it and a method for including it in your course assessment. CARRY IT OUT if the class votes to use your idea and DEBRIEF on its strengths and weaknesses.	2. ANNOUNCE a pop-quiz. GAUGE students' response. DISCUSS pros and cons of testing in this manner as well as in other ways. 3. GIVE students a test (like "HOW IT WORKS" on p. 57). DISCUSS the strengths and weaknesses therein.

Chapter 14: Checking Your Understanding

Match the following terms with your own definitions or summary statements taken from the text:

reliability	criterion-referenced test	content validity	validity
accuracy	concurrent validity	norm-referenced test	standardized tests

True or False:

1._____Generally, the more items included in a test, the higher the test's reliability.
2._____An advantage to "grading on the curve" is that it simplifies marking decisions.
3._____The purpose of a test blueprint is to create a format for grading future tests—saving a teacher time and effort in writing tests.
4._____Equal differences between percentile ranks indicate equal differences in achievement.
5._____One way to reduce the effects of guessing on True/False tests is to require students to correct false items to make them true.
6._____When standardized tests originated, it was widely believed that learning ability was inherited, fixed, and largely unchangeable. As a result, tests were constructed and interpreted in ways some current educators question.
7._____A good practice for giving essay tests is to write many essay questions and allow students to choose one they want to answer—enhancing a sense of choice and self-expression.
8._____Teachers should avoid using controversial items on essay tests because there is no single right answer.

1. T   2. T   3. F   4. F   5. T   6. T   7. F   8. F

Chapter 14: Performance Assessment Ideas

Individual	Small Group	Whole Class
1. INTERVIEW an instructor about the kinds of tests s/he uses and why. ASK for pointers helpful to a beginning teacher. SUMMARIZE the results of your interview and LINK them to the material discussed for this chapter and/or in your course text.	1. FIND an old objective test from this course or another—or OBTAIN a test used in the grade level/subject you'd like to teach. EVALUATE the questions for variety and effectiveness. What do you notice?	1. OBTAIN a copy of a standardized test (practice form) used in elementary or secondary schools in your area. As a class, "TAKE" the test and then EVALUATE both the experience and the questions. CONSIDER the types of questions and their validity. What RECOMMENDATIONS would you make regarding the use of this test?

REFERENCES

Educational Leadership. (1994, October). 52, (2).
  Entire issue is dedicated to assessment.

Farr, Roger. (1992). Putting it all together: Solving the reading assessment puzzle. *The Reading Teacher.* **46, (1), 26-37.**
  Noted assessment authority offers a short history of assessment in the United States and summarizes the numerous considerations involved in assessment, including assessment audience, purposes, etc.

Glazer, Susan Mandel. (1993, January). Assessment in the classroom: Where we are, where we're going. *Teaching: K-8.* **68-71.**
  Discusses the debate over assessment and the role of standardized testing in the schools. Advocates creating a balance between various elements involved in assessment.

Glazer, Susan Mandel. (1993, February). Authentic assessment. *Teaching: K-8.* **99-100.**
  Offers guidance for teachers who want to enhance their assessment skills for a better match between curriculum and testing.

Winograd, Peter; Paris, Scott; & Bridge, Connie. (1991). Improving the assessment of literacy. *The Reading Teacher.* **45, (2), 108-116.**
  Explains many of the disadvantages of traditional assessments and offers several guidelines to improve assessment.

BRIDGES

Chapter 15
Assessing Learners: Performance Assessment

KNOWLEDGE — **ACTIVITY**

Chapter 15	A. Personal, Dialogue, or Buddy Journals	B. Self-Directed Study Activities	C. Cooperative & Collaborative Ideas	D. Whole Class
Introducing the Content	1. What comes to mind when you hear the term "performance assessment?" Have you been involved in any performance assessment? What do you see as pros and cons from a learning perspective? From a teaching perspective? 2. How do you feel about grades? Tests? How would/could you alter the system?	1. WRITE a personal philosophy statement as if for a job application on your philosophy of teaching, learning, discipline, and management. CONSIDER especially issues of assessment: How do you plan to ascertain what students know and what they accomplish? 2. ASSESS yourself on one of the assessments in the referenced articles, or on some areas you choose, such as: acquiring information, organizing it, and using it. What implications do these skills have for your teaching career?	1. When should you assess learning? (i.e., before, during, after a lesson, unit, etc.). Why do you feel this way?	1. INTRODUCE this chapter with the following quotation: Give me a fish and I eat for a day. Teach me to fish and I eat for a lifetime. —Author Unknown. ASK how a teacher can know a child has learned something. CONTRAST a performance assessment with a paper/pencil test. MAKE THE CASE that testing "how to fish" would be best carried out at a stream with a rod, rather than the in a classroom with a paper/pencil test.

97

Chapter 15 Continued	A. Personal, Dialogue, or Buddy Journals	B. Self-Directed Study Activities	C. Cooperative & Collaborative Ideas	D. Whole Class
Assimilating /Reviewing the Content	3. Who should be involved in performance assessment? What do you think should be collected? By whom? Why? When? How often? 4. When should you assess learning? (i.e., before, during, after a lesson, unit, etc.). Why do you feel this way?	3. CREATE a self-evaluation rubric related to a particular area of knowledge/expertise you hope to develop or have developed in this course. EXPLAIN why this process is helpful. 4. COMPLETE a self-evaluation rubric if you've been keeping a portfolio for this course. Where are your major areas of growth? Where would you like to improve? What kinds of learning experiences appear to be particularly useful to you? Why? What implications does this have for your future teaching decisions?	2. BRAINSTORM a rubric for grading the portfolios being used in this class (if that option was chosen). If a rubric already exists, REVIEW IT and SUGGEST alterations/changes. NEGOTIATE these changes with the other groups and the course instructor. 3. BRAINSTORM some performance assessments that could be pertinent to this course. What are the strengths and weaknesses of these ideas? If possible, COMPLETE some of these ideas.	2. DISCUSS primary trait and/or holistic scoring procedures. Work as a group to score some student essays (obtained from a nearby elementary school perhaps). DEBRIEF on the experience.

Chapter 15: Checking Your Understanding

Match the following terms with your own definitions or summary statements taken from the text:

rating scales	portfolio assessment	performance assessment	rubric
primary trait scoring	objective assessment	holistic scoring	checklists

True or False:

1. _____ When creating a scoring system for a performance assessment, the number of points or categories should be limited for ease of use and scoring.
2. _____ It is important to remember that performance assessments are tests and that no learning should occur during the assessment.
3. _____ An area conventional tests have assessed very well over the years is that of student affect and attitude.
4. _____ A well-planned performance assessment presents the learner with an authentic, real-world problem or challenge.
5. _____ Conventional paper-pencil tests are popular because they measure learning directly.
6. _____ One advantage of performance assessment is that it can be used at any point in the instruction process without losing its usefulness.

Multiple Choice:

7. Which of the following is **not** a common test constraint to be considered in creating performance assessments?
   a. time to prepare, revise, finish
   b. equipment such as calculators, computers, etc.
   c. getting help from others
   d. cost of reference materials

    1. T   2. F   3. F   4. T   5. F   6. T   7. d

Chapter 15: Performance Assessment Ideas

Individual	Small Group	Whole Class
1. COMPLETE the final self-evaluation of your portfolio if you have been keeping one during this course. MEET with your instructor to evaluate your progress in the course and the value of the portfolio experience.	1. If you have been keeping portfolios, BRING them to class and SHARE your favorite entries. DISCUSS the value of the portfolios as well as suggestions for improvement.	1. Ask students to WRITE a summary of their teaching philosophy and management plans. EXPLAIN to students that this summary is similar to an essay question on many job applications forms, making this writing a "real world" experience. STATE evaluation criteria clearly before students write—are there concepts or areas they MUST address? Is form/mechanics focus a part of the scoring? Etc.

REFERENCES

Anderson, Jeffrey B. & Freiberg, H. Jerome. (1995). Using self-assessment as a reflective tool to enhance the student-teaching experience. *Teacher Education Quarterly.* 22, (1), 77-91.
Discusses the value of helping prospective teachers reflect on and evaluate their own performance just as we encourage them to require of their students.

Asturias, Harold. (1994). Using students' portfolios to assess mathematical understanding. *The Mathematics Teacher.* 87, (9), 698-701.
Discusses why and how to use portfolios in mathematics assessment.

Berenson, Sarah B. & Carter, Glenda S. (1995). Changing assessment practices in science and mathematics. *School Science and Mathematics.* 95, (4), 182-186.
Describes use of journals, portfolios, and performance assessment activities.

Cutting, Brian (No date). *Getting started in whole language.* Washington: The Wright Group Inc. (ISBN 1-55911-041-4).
Offers ideas for reading and writing instruction/evaluation in elementary classrooms (from a holistic perspective). Includes possible first day schedules and activities.

Eggleton, Jill. (1990). *Whole language evaluation.* Washington: The Wright Group Inc. (ISBN 962-291-440-3)
Hands-on approach to evaluation of elementary children's reading, writing, and spelling from a whole language perspective.

Farr, Roger & Greene, Beth. (1993). Improving reading assessments: Understanding the social and political agenda for testing. *Educational Horizons.* 72, (1), 20-27.
Provides a brief history of the evolution of testing to help readers understand current criticism of some of these techniques. Includes a brief recommendation section.

Henk, William A. & Melnick, Steven A. (1995). The Reader Self-Perception Scale (RSPS): A new tool for measuring how children feel about themselves as readers. *The Reading Teacher.* 48, (6), 470-482.
Introduces an instrument for assessing readers' self-perceptions and sense of self-efficacy, targeted particularly for primary and intermediate level students.

Johnston, Peter H., (Ed.). (1992). Snow White and the seven warnings: Threats to authentic evaluation. *The Reading Teacher.* 46, (3), 250-252.
Suggests seven areas where assessment can be misleading or confusing.

Kirby, D. & T. Liner. (1981). *Inside out: Developmental strategies for teaching writing.* Upper Montclair, New Jersey: Boynton/Cook Publishers, 191-193.
Provides a discussion on the use of the Diedrich Scale for evaluating student writing.

Kuhs, Therese M. 91994). Portfolio assessment: Making it work for the first time. *The Mathematics Teacher.* 87, (5), 332-335.
Offers step-by-step considerations for undertaking portfolio assessment.

McKenna, Michael C. & Kear, Dennis J. (1990). Measuring attitude toward reading: A new tool for teachers. *The Reading Teacher.* 43, (9), 626-639.
Offers a fun instrument for measuring children's reading attitude for academic and recreational reading which is normed for grades 1-6.

Rhodes, Lynn K & Nathenson-Mejia, Sally. (1992). Anecdotal records: A powerful tool for ongoing literacy assessment. *The Reading Teacher.* 45, (7), 502-509.
Describes the usefulness of anecdotal records and offers suggestions for using them successfully in assessment.

Sgroi, Laura A.; Gropper, Nancy; Kilker, Mary Fom; Rambusch, Nancy M.; & Semonite, Barbara. (1995). Assessing young children's mathematical understandings. *Teaching Children Mathematics.* **1,** (5), 275-277.
Describes how teachers devised assessment activities to coincide with the teaching activities they were using.

Stahle, Debra L. & Mitchell, Judith P. (1993). Portfolio assessment in college methods courses: Practicing what we preach. *Journal of Reading.* **36,** (7), 538-542.
Offers suggestions for using portfolios in college methods classes so future teachers can experience this alternative assessment practice from the "inside".

Tierney, R., Carter, M., & Desai, L. (1991). *Portfolio assessment in the reading-writing classroom.* Norwood, Massachusetts: Christopher Gordon.
A complete book on portfolio assessment which examines pros and cons of the approach and offers concrete suggestions for making portfolio assessment useful and effective.

Wilson, Linda. (1994). What gets graded is what gets valued. *The Mathematics Teacher.* **87,** (6), 412-414.
Suggests that students tend to avoid class activities that don't "count" toward their grades.